The

ESV

and the

ENGLISH BIBLE

LEGACY

❦

LELAND RYKEN

"Leland Ryken brilliantly demonstrates historically and linguistically that Bible translation philosophy is a life and death matter, and that it takes a thorough commitment to producing an 'essentially literal' translation to convey (and not obscure) the multiplex, polychrome fullness of God's Word. Unflinching. Powerful. Convincing."

R. Kent Hughes, Senior Pastor Emeritus, College Church, Wheaton, Illinois

"In this fascinating book, one of the world's most renowned experts on the literary qualities of the Bible explains what made the King James Version of 1611 the standard of translation excellence for centuries, and shows convincingly how the ESV and several other modern versions compare favorably or unfavorably to that enduring standard. An excellent book for understanding why translations differ, and why it is important."

Wayne Grudem, Research Professor of Theology and Biblical Studies, Phoenix Seminary

"Every generation has to fight their own 'battle for the Bible.' Today the issue is seen through the 'What does this mean to you?' syndrome, an aversion to propositions, and most recently, the questioning of the historicity of Genesis. That's why *The ESV and the English Bible Legacy* is so critical. In the current climate of pop Bible translations it is critical to have a translation like the ESV, which is faithful to the original text, honors the traditional treasures of literary style and readability, and is widely accessible. Last year we began using the ESV officially in our church and sold over two thousand Bibles in our church bookstore, most of which were ESVs. Obviously, we believe in the legacy Dr. Ryken explains in this book!"

Jon McNeff, Senior Pastor, NorthCreek Church, Walnut Creek, California

The
ESV
and the
ENGLISH BIBLE
LEGACY

The

ESV

and the

ENGLISH BIBLE
LEGACY

LELAND RYKEN

WHEATON, ILLINOIS

The ESV and the English Bible Legacy

Copyright © 2011 by Leland Ryken

Published by Crossway
       1300 Crescent Street
       Wheaton, Illinois 60187

Cover design: Studio Gearbox

Cover photo: Corbis Images

Page design and typesetting: Dawn Premako

First printing 2011

Printed in the United States of America

Scriptures marked as "(cev)" are taken from the Contemporary English Version Copyright © 1995 by American Bible Society. Used by permission.

Scripture quotations marked esv are from the ESV® Bible (*The Holy Bible, English Standard Version*®), copyright © 2001 by Crossway Bibles. Used by permission. All rights reserved.

Scripture quotations marked hcsb have been taken from *The Holman Christian Standard Bible*®. Copyright © 1999, 2000, 2002, 2003 by Holman Bible Publishers. Used by permission.

Scripture quotations marked kjv are from the *King James Version* of the Bible.

Scripture quotations marked nasb are from *The New American Standard Bible*®. Copyright © The Lockman Foundation 1960, 1962, 1963, 1968, 1971, 1972, 1973, 1975, 1977. Used by permission.

Scripture quotations marked ncv are from *The Holy Bible, New Century Version*, copyright © 1987, 1988, 1991 by Word Publishing, Dallas, Texas 75039. Used by permission.

Scripture references marked neb are from *The New English Bible* © The Delegates of the Oxford University Press and The Syndics of the Cambridge University Press, 1961, 1970.

Scripture references marked niv are taken from *The Holy Bible, New International Version*®, NIV®. Copyright © 1973, 1978, 1984, 2011 by Biblica, Inc.™ Used by permission. All rights reserved worldwide.

Scripture references marked nkjv are from *The New King James Version*. Copyright © 1982, Thomas Nelson, Inc. Used by permission.

Scripture references marked nlt are from *The Holy Bible, New Living Translation*, copyright © 1996, 2004. Used by permission of Tyndale House Publishers, Inc., Wheaton, Ill., 60189. All rights reserved.

Scripture references marked rsv are from *The Revised Standard Version*. Copyright © 1946, 1952, 1971, 1973 by the Division of Christian Education of the National Council of the Churches of Christ in the U.S.A.

Trade paperback ISBN: 978-1-4335-3066-1
PDF ISBN: 978-1-4335-3067-8
Mobipocket ISBN: 978-1-4335-3068-5
ePub ISBN: 978-1-4335-3069-2

Library of Congress Cataloging-in-Publication Data
Ryken, Leland.
  The ESV and the English Bible legacy / Leland Ryken.
    p. cm.
  ISBN 978-1-4335-3066-1 (tp)
  1. Bible. English—Versions—English Standard. 2. Bible.
English—Versions—History.
I. Title.

  BS195.E642R95 2011

  220.5'208—dc23   2011026423

For
Sharon and Norm Ewert
Wayne and Nita Martindale

CONTENTS

Part Three: The English Standard Version: Heir to the Great Tradition

ABBREVIATIONS OF
BIBLE VERSIONS

CEV	Contemporary English Version
ESV	English Standard Version
GNB	Good News Bible (Today's English Version)
HCSB	Holman Christian Standard Bible
JB	Jerusalem Bible
KJV	King James Version
NASB	New American Standard Bible
NCV	New Century Version
NEB	New English Bible
NIV	New International Version
NKJV	New King James Version
NLT	New Living Translation
NLV	New Life Version
REB	Revised English Bible
RSV	Revised Standard Version

PREFACE

The purpose of this book is to keep the nature and excellence of the English Standard Version (ESV) of the Bible in public view. The ESV was published in 2001 and has grown in influence ever since. But the crosswinds of Bible translation controversy that swirl around us make it continuously necessary to explain why the ESV deserves to be the Bible of choice.

I have written extensively on the subject of Bible translation philosophy, using the ESV as well as other translations to illustrate various aspects of essentially literal Bible translation. This book differs from my previous books and essays in two respects. First, this time I have not written primarily to explain and defend a translation philosophy but to delineate the nature of the English Standard Version of the Bible. Second, having written a book on the King James Bible, it became apparent to me that I can achieve the purpose stated above by placing the ESV into the context of English Bible translation from its beginning to the present day.

This explains the format that I use in this book. I will begin by describing "the classic mainstream of English Bible translations," a phrase from the preface to the ESV. Then I will show how the ESV perpetuates that tradition, in contrast to the branch of modern translations known as dynamic equivalent translations. Implicit in my approach is the premise that part of the greatness of the ESV is the greatness of the tradition to which it belongs.

PART ONE

The Classic Mainstream of English Bible Translation

1

THE TRANSLATIONS THAT
MAKE UP THE TRADITION

When the translation committee of the Revised Standard Version (1952) composed its preface, it spoke of "the great Tyndale–King James tradition." The preface to the New Revised Standard Version (1989) likewise identifies something called "the great tradition of the King James Bible and its predecessors." And the preface to the English Standard Version (ESV; 2001) speaks of "the Tyndale–King James legacy." The purpose of this chapter is to flesh out what these phrases mean.

Four things are worthy of note at the outset: (1) The tradition consists of multiple English translations of the Bible. (2) These individual translations have so much in common that they constitute a single tradition, distinct from alternatives that emerged along the way, beginning with the Revised Version (1885) and accelerating with the rise of dynamic equivalent translations in the middle of the twentieth century. (3) This family of translations was dominant from Wycliffite beginnings (ca. 1380) right through the middle of the twentieth century. (4) The King James Version (KJV; 1611) was the final codification of preceding translations, and it became the channel through which the tradition maintained its dominance, explaining why the tradition is always identified with the KJV.

THE HEADWATERS

The great tradition begins not with William Tyndale but a century and a half earlier with John Wycliffe ("morning star of the Reformation," as he is called). Wycliffe's translation is more accurately called the Wycliffite translation, because it was chiefly the work of Wycliffe's associates rather than Wycliffe himself. Additionally, it is important to know that the Wycliffite translators actually produced two versions of the Bible: one a literal translation from the Latin Vulgate and a second translation that had more of an eye on the English receptor language than on Latin, which in this case was the donor language. The complete Bible appeared around 1380.

It might seem unnecessary to push the great tradition back to Wycliffe. For one thing, Wycliffe's language was Middle English—the language of Chaucer but not what is called modern language (the language of Tyndale and Shakespeare, despite its archaisms by the standard of modern usage). Second, there were no printed versions of the Wycliffite Bible until the middle of the nineteenth century. This means that all versions in Wycliffe's lifetime were handwritten manuscript copies, disseminated partly by oral readings conducted by traveling preachers known as Lollards.

But there are other factors that make it necessary to trace the great tradition back to Wycliffe. The foundation of the tradition was simply the demonstration that the Bible could be translated into English. To cite a parallel, modern jet travel would never have happened if the Wright brothers had not flown a rudimentary aircraft at Kitty Hawk in 1903. A historian of English Bible translation correctly asserts that "the Wycliffe Bible was . . . not merely a book but an event, . . . [marking] a momentous epoch in our religious development."[1]

Additionally, once the Wycliffite Bibles began to make the rounds, they created a grassroots thirst among Englishmen to have access to the Bible in the vernacular. Even today, the Wycliffite translation survives in a staggering total of 250 manuscripts, more than any other medieval English text.[2] Only the wealthy could hope to afford a manuscript copy of the Wycliffite Bible, but farmers were willing to give a load of hay in exchange for a day's use of a copy.[3] A Bible-hungry readership did not suddenly appear in William Tyndale's time; ferment for an English Bible had been around for a long time.

How the Headwaters Become a River

John Wycliffe can be considered the pioneer of English Bible translation, but in terms of direct influence on the English Bibles that we hold in our hands today, William Tyndale's printed work is the place where foreshadowings became a mighty stream. Educated at Oxford University, Tyndale (1494–1536) was a linguistic genius who was conversant in at least seven languages. His doctrinal convictions made him an early Reformer. His particular zeal as a Reformer was translating the Bible from the original languages into English, a passion that he came to view as his life calling.

Because Tyndale's religious views were condemned as heretical by the Catholic Church, Tyndale carried out his work of translation on the Continent under threat to his life. He worked in a largely solitary manner. The specific qualities of Tyndale's translation that he bequeathed to the tradition that followed will be noted in later chapters. The important point here is the revolution that the English Bible effected in English life. Copies of Tyndale's New Testament were published in 1525 and reached England in the following year. Because the Bible was a banned book, it had to be smuggled into England in sacks of flour and bales of cloth. Book burnings by Catholic bishops did not stem the flood.

There are two dimensions to the revolution that the Tyndale New Testament started in England. One is that it created a religious change in which people read the Bible voraciously as the very Word of God and therefore based their doctrine and lifestyle on what the Bible said. David Daniell paints the following picture of the appetite for the vernacular Bible that Tyndale helped to create: "There is no shortage of evidence of the gatherings of people of all ages, all over the country, to read and hear these English Scriptures—and reading meant, so often, reading aloud. . . . The corner that English readers turned in the 1530s . . . did not lead to one or two curious Bible effects. . . . On the contrary: turning that corner was suddenly to be faced with a vast, rich, sunlit territory."[4] No publishing venture succeeds without a readership. Tyndale's New Testament created a Bible-reading public in England.

There is also a linguistic dimension to the revolution created by Tyndale. Before Tyndale's time, most of the important religious and intellectual business in England and in Europe had been conducted in Latin. Tyndale's work of translation struck a blow for the English vernacular. Tyndale's English, moreover, although it is today so archaic that many refer to it as "old English," is technically modern English. David Daniell claims that Tyndale bequeathed a plain style to the English language, with *plain* meaning "clear," not low or colloquial.[5]

TWO FALLACIES ABOUT TYNDALE THE TRANSLATOR

The debt that the classic mainstream of English Bible translation owes to Tyndale is obvious and well established by scholars. We can agree with the verdict that "the work of William Tyndale should be valued as the greatest influence on English translations and its language."[6] Yet some glibness in this regard will obscure the nature of the great tradition if left unchallenged.

Fallacy 1: Tyndale aimed his translation at an illiterate or nonreading public. The source of this misconception is a famous incident that has been extravagantly misinterpreted. The incident is as follows, as recounted in John Foxe's *Book of Martyrs*:

> There dwelt not far off a certain doctor, that had been chancellor to a bishop, who had been of old, familiar acquaintance with Master Tyndale . . . unto whom Master Tyndale went and opened his mind upon diverse questions of the Scripture: for to him he durst be bold to disclose his heart. Unto whom the doctor said, "Do you not know that the pope is very Antichrist, whom the Scripture speaketh of? But beware what you say; for if you shall be perceived to be of that opinion, it will cost you your life."
>
> Not long after, Master Tyndale happened to be in the company of a certain divine, recounted for a learned man, and, in communing and disputing with him, he drove him to that issue, that the said great doctor burst out into these blasphemous words, "We were better to be without God's laws than the pope's." Master Tyndale, hearing this, full of godly zeal, and not bearing that blasphemous saying, replied, "I defy the pope, and all his laws;" and added, "If God spared him life, ere many years he would cause a boy that driveth the plough to know more of the Scripture than he did."[7]

We should note first what is *not* going on here. The statement about the plowboy is not a comment about Tyndale's preferred style for an English Bible. It is not a designation of teenage farm boys as a target audience for a niche Bible. Those misconceptions are the projections of modern partisans for a colloquial and simplified English Bible.

21

Foxe's account makes it clear that the subject of debate at this early stage of Tyndale's career (before he had even begun to translate the Bible) was the question of papal authority versus scriptural authority. When the priest asserted a strong view of papal authority and denigrated the authority of the Bible, Tyndale responded by making an implied case for the Bible as the authority for Christian belief and conduct. The background is Tyndale's growing agitation at the prevailing Catholic ignorance of the Bible. This explains the specific thing that Tyndale said to the priest, namely, that he wanted English Christians to know "more of the Scripture" than a Catholic knew. A Catholic would have known only as much Scripture as appeared in church rituals (chiefly the Mass), and he would have known it in Latin rather than English.

Second, the reference to the plowboy is not a comment about a social class toward which Tyndale slanted his translation. It is instead a comment about how widely Tyndale wanted the English Bible to be disseminated in English society. Tyndale was not making a bow to farm boys. He was using a particular example to make the general point that he wanted the whole cross section of the English population to have access to the Bible.

Fallacy 2: Tyndale was in favor of a colloquial English style for Bible translations. The culprit here is a few famous colloquialisms in Tyndale's translation that have (again) been seized upon by modern readers who prefer a colloquial English Bible to a dignified one. The two most famous instances of Tyndale's daring are the following: When the Serpent replies to Eve's protest that she cannot eat the forbidden fruit because if she does she will die, Tyndale has the Serpent reply, "Tush, ye shall not die" (Gen. 3:4). And instead of saying that Joseph was successful in Potiphar's house, Tyndale said that he "was a lucky fellow" (Gen. 39:2).

In later chapters I will explore Tyndale's style in greater detail. For now it is enough to say that Tyndale's prevailing style is not accurately represented by occasional flourishes such as the ones noted. Enthusiasts for Tyndale's translation regularly make a contradictory claim. On the one hand, they want the world to know that in the parts of the Bible that Tyndale translated, upwards of 80 percent of his renderings made their way into the KJV. Most of these same partisans then set up Tyndale and the King James translators as opponents on the question of style, claiming that Tyndale was colloquial and racy, while the KJV is formal.

It cannot be both ways. Tyndale cannot be both the predecessor that the King James translators scrupulously followed and their great opponent in regard to style. The fact is that Tyndale, while less formal than the KJV, nonetheless is in the same lexical and syntactic range. Here is Tyndale's translation of the opening lines of Jesus's Sermon on the Mount: "When he saw the people he went up into a mountain, and when he was set, his disciples came to him, and he opened his mouth, and taught them saying: Blessed are the poor in spirit, for theirs is the kingdom of heaven. Blessed are they that mourn, for they shall be comforted. Blessed are the meek, for they shall inherit the earth. Blessed are they which hunger and thirst for righteousness, for they shall be filled" (Matt. 5:1–6). Anyone familiar with the King James rendition can see at once that the two are nearly the same. It is equally evident that Tyndale did not lower the style to match the way the local plowboy talked.

THE RIVER WIDENS: BETWEEN TYNDALE AND THE KJV

It is customary to name the mainstream tradition "the Tyndale–King James" tradition. This is not a wholly happy situation, for two reasons. First, it is an ambiguous designation. Does it name (1) the two translations that constitute the tradition or (2) the first and last translations of a sixteenth-century tradition that included five major translations between those two translations? Additionally, the Tyndale–King James label arbitrarily elevates Tyndale over other sixteenth-century translations. Virtually all scholarly sources claim that the Geneva Bible contributed more to the King James Version than did Tyndale (and we should note in this regard that Tyndale translated less than two-thirds of the Bible).

Five translations constitute the "middle" of the story of sixteenth-century English Bible translations of which Tyndale and the KJV form the first and last chapters. Later I will explore their contributions in more detail; the external facts are as follows:

Coverdale's Bible (1535)

Miles Coverdale had been an associate of Tyndale on the Continent. Unlike Tyndale, he did not read Hebrew and Greek. Nonetheless, he had a more diplomatic temperament than Tyndale, living to the age of eighty-one and working on a total of three English translations. Additionally, he was an English stylist par excellence, as Tyndale was a linguist. Coverdale's Bible was the first complete Bible in modern English and the first to receive the king's approval.

Matthew's Bible (1537)

Matthew was the pen name of John Rogers, and his translation shares much in common with Coverdale's Bible: it is a one-man translation, and Rogers, too, had been an associate of Tyndale. Like Coverdale's Bible, Matthew's Bible enjoyed ecclesiastical and royal sanction.

The Great Bible (1539)

We should pause to note what a steamroller of momentum English Bible translation experienced in the 1530s. Every two years saw the publication of a new English translation. The designation Great Bible is not honorific but instead comes from the massive size and weight of the book. The Great Bible was the first sixteenth-century translation produced by a committee, and it was the first to be named the official Bible of the Church of England.

The Geneva Bible (1560)

Like Tyndale's translation, the Geneva Bible was produced on the Continent (in Geneva, Switzerland). Also like Tyndale's translation, it was produced by radical Protestants known as Puritans (the English branch of the Protestant Reformation). If the Great Bible was the Bible of the established Church of England, the Geneva Bible served an alternate constituency and has always been informally known as the Puritan Bible.

The Bishops' Bible (1568)

This was a protest Bible instigated by Queen Elizabeth to counter the Puritan aspects of the popular Geneva Bible. It is called the Bishops' Bible because all of the translation was done by Anglican bishops, and it was another ecclesiastical translation whose use was mandated within the Church of England (but not with a Bible-reading public that could choose its own translation).

Summing Up

Tyndale's influence continued after his martyrdom, but if other translators had not continued his work, we would not have had the English Bible as we know it. Furthermore, it is unlikely that the flurry of Bible publication that has been described above would have occurred without the impetus of new translations.

THE CLIMAX OF SIXTEENTH-CENTURY TRANSLATION: THE KING JAMES VERSION OF 1611

The King James Version (1611) was a definitive codification of the preceding seven English translations (Wycliffe, Tyndale, and the five succeeding ones). As will be noted in later chapters, each of the preceding translations contributed to the King James Bible. One of the quirks is that of all the predecessors, the Bishops' Bible contributed least of its own phraseology, yet it was the stipulated starting point for the work of the King James translators. The significance of the King James Bible is not its innovations but its synthesis of all that was best in the preceding tradition. This is not to deny that "compared with its predecessors, the King James version shows a superb faculty of selection and combination, a sure instinct for betterment."[8]

For purposes of this chapter, what matters most is that the KJV became the channel that preserved the mainstream tradition for three centuries. The KJV was *the* Bible of the English-speaking world throughout that long interval. In fact, the KJV was what people meant when they spoke of "the Bible." Contrary to the claims of debunkers, the KJV achieved that prominence relatively quickly. It supplanted the best-selling Geneva Bible within fifty years. Although the King James Bible was never officially authorized by an ecclesiastical or civic body (hence the irony of the common nomenclature "Authorized Version"), it received an even better authorization. In the words of one scholar, the King James Bible "was authorized, not by an edict imposed upon the people, but by popular acclamation" as "a book whose excellence was admitted on all sides."[9]

There are two ways to document the virtual monopoly that the King James Bible exercised as the surviving exemplar of the classic tradition. One is to explore its influence on English-speaking society in all spheres, as I did in my book *The Legacy of the King James Bible*.[10] The other way is to observe the failed attempts to displace the KJV even when it started to show its age. The most dramatic example is the sensational appearance of the Revised Version. When the Revised Version's New Testament hit the streets of London in 1881, the streets around the publishing house were blocked from dawn to dusk with processions of wagons being loaded with Bibles for transport. Leading newspapers in the United States had the text telegraphed for serial printing, and the new translation sold three hundred thousand copies the first day it was available in New York City. But after the dust had settled, the King James Version did not have its supremacy undermined at all.

SUMMARY

Designations such as the Tyndale–King James tradition and "the classic mainstream of English Bible translation" are not vacuous, honorific, flag-waving labels. We can identify exactly what translations make up that tradition. Even though we need to keep the record clear as to what various translations contributed to the growing stream, we also have the convenience of knowing that the final translation in the process—the King James Version of 1611—is the definitive codification of the tradition and the channel through which it maintained its supremacy for more than three centuries.

Additionally, it is not open to dispute that this was the leading tradition from 1525 to 1970. This means that if we identify the translation philosophy and style of the King James tradition (the subject of subsequent chapters), it will be obvious that modern dynamic equivalent translations have no claim to prominence in the history of English Bible translation as a whole. Dynamic equivalence is a recent arrival and a distinct departure from what had prevailed for six centuries, starting with John Wycliffe in the latter fourteenth century.

2

How the Bible Was Viewed

Modern Bible translation has become such a technical and sophisticated discipline that it is easy for us to start thinking of it as a set of techniques and "tools." What a translator believes about the nature of the Bible has correspondingly come to count for less than it once did—doubly and triply so when a translator's view of Scripture is paired with a willingness to dispense with the actual words of biblical authors. Stated another way: when we come to evaluate a modern translation, we mainly need to know the translation philosophy on which the committee has operated, not what the translators believe about the Bible.

This is in contrast to the first English translators of the Bible. What these translators believed about Scripture governed how they translated the Bible. In the prefaces to some (but not all) modern translations, the customary paragraph assuring readers that all committee members embrace an evangelical view of the Bible as God's Word has little implication for the actual translation. For Wycliffe, Tyndale, and their heirs, the translators' view of Scripture determined virtually everything.

THE REFORMATION CONTEXT

The attitude of the early translators toward the Bible sprang from their moment in the history of Christendom. The great battle of the Reformation era focused on the question of religious authority. The longstanding Catholic tradition gave somewhat equal weight to the Bible, the pope, and church tradition. Certainly there had been no concept of "Scripture alone" as the foundation for faith and practice.

Along came the Protestant Reformation; for its adherents the Bible alone was the final authority. Tremendous weight was attached to having access to the Bible and knowing what it actually said, not what was doled out in a Latin Mass or referenced in Latin choral texts. If we return for a moment to the famous statement by Tyndale about the plowboy, the context was not a debate about the target audience of a niche Bible or the right style for an English Bible but the question of scriptural authority and the resultant conviction that people needed access to the Bible in their own language.

What we are to picture is a whole climate in which English Bible translation took place. When the Bible ceased to be a banned book in England, the ferment of interest in reading and hearing the Bible in English was breathtaking. Here is how a contemporary of Thomas Cranmer described the situation:

> It was wonderful to see with what joy the book of God was received, not only among the learneder sort and those that were noted for lovers of the reformation, but generally all England over among all the vulgar and common people; with what greediness God's word was read, and what resort to places where the reading of it was. Everybody that could bought the book and busily read it; or got others to read it to them, if they could not themselves; and diverse among the elderly learned to read on purpose. And

even little boys flocked among the rest to hear portions of the
Holy Scriptures read.[1]

The Bible was obviously elevated to a position of unprecedented
centrality in people's daily religious experience, and it also elicited
unprecedented reverence and esteem.

THE BIBLE AS GOD'S WORD

Within the Reformation milieu that I have pictured, people had
an extraordinary sense of the Bible as God's Word. The Bible was
a one-of-a-kind book—a divine rather than human book. The
words of the Bible were received as the words of God. I do not have
time to explore the way in which the Reformation era formulated
a doctrine of the plenary inspiration of Scripture (the belief that
the words and not just the thoughts of the Bible were given by
God), but this doctrine (also called verbal inspiration) was in full
force as the translations that make up the mainstream tradition
were produced.[2]

Within such a view of the Bible as God's Word, translators
did not feel free to tamper with the words of Scripture as they
translated. The preface to the Geneva Bible spells this out. The
translators explained that they had "in every point *and word* . . .
faithfully rendered the text." Further, the translators "endeavored
to set forth the purity *of the word*" found in the Bible. And again,
"We most reverently kept the propriety *of the words*" (italics added).

The preface to the King James Version ("The Translators to the
Reader") is equally instructive on this point. The preface criticizes
"the Seventy" (the translation committee that produced the Sep-
tuagint) for sometimes being "interpreters" instead of translators.
"They did many things well," states the preface, but they were also
guilty of license at some points: "sometimes they may be noted to
add to the Original, and sometimes to take from it."

A whole view of the translator is implied by such a passage. For the King James committee, a translator of the Bible is a steward who oversees something that is entrusted to him. Or the translator is like a messenger from a king whose task is to convey what the king has said. What a translator is *not*, according to this line of thinking, is an editor and/or commentator who is free to massage the text, adding something here and omitting something there.

THE GOAL OF BIBLE TRANSLATION

If we come to the prefaces of premodern English Bible translations with the expectations of our own day, we can scarcely avoid being perplexed. Modern conventions have led us to expect a clear delineation of translation philosophy, of Hebrew and Greek manuscripts favored by the committee, of Hebrew and Greek lexicons consulted, and perhaps of a target audience named. As long as the mainstream tradition was in the ascendancy, these matters received scant or no attention in English Bible prefaces.

The primary stated goal in the older translations was solidly evangelical and evangelistic. The translators wanted readers to understand and believe the gospel and thus secure the eternal salvation of their souls. This keynote was already sounded by the translators of the Wycliffite Bible. Wycliffe's associate John Purvey wrote in the prologue, "May God grant to us all the grace to know well and fully obey the holy scriptures."[3] Another associate wrote that the purpose of the translation was "to save all men in our realm whom God will have saved."[4] This theme is greatly amplified in Tyndale's preface to his New Testament, which is a multipage outline of the Christian doctrine of sin and salvation.

The preface to the King James Bible likewise states a spiritual goal for Bible translation. Here is an excerpt:

It remaineth, that we commend thee to God, and to the Spirit of his grace, which is able to build further than we can ask or think. He removeth the scales from our eyes, the veil from our hearts, opening our wits that we may understand his word, enlarging our hearts, yea correcting our affections, that we may love it above gold and silver, yea that we may love it to the end. Ye are brought unto fountains of living water which ye digged not. . . . Others have laboured, and you may enter into their labours; O receive not so great things in vain, O despise not so great salvation! . . . It is a fearful thing to fall into the hands of the living God; but a blessed thing it is, and will bring us to everlasting blessedness in the end, when God speaketh unto us, to hearken; when he setteth his word before us, to read it; when he stretcheth out his hand and calleth, to answer, Here am I, here we are to do thy will, O God.

I have long believed that the concluding paragraphs of evangelical Bible translations, right to the present day, make some of the best devotional reading available.

This, then, is the evangelistic goal of translation for the early English Bible translators. If we think that this is not directly related to the translation practices of the translators, we are wrong. The translators approached their work as a life-or-death matter. Accuracy was not judged by the same criteria as governed the translation of Homer or Plato. Translators of the latter did not express a wish that their readers would obey their authors for the salvation of their souls.

PRACTICAL IMPLICATIONS OF HOW TRANSLATORS VIEW THE BIBLE

I can imagine that some of my readers will have been thinking that my description of the Reformation era is the same as what we find in evangelical circles today and among evangelical translators. After all, don't those people believe that the Bible is God's Word? I believe that this theoretic agreement between Christians then and now actually conceals unbridgeable differences.

Consider the typical church situation. As a combined group, attendees at church services and small group meetings carry four or five or six different English translations of the Bible. These vary widely from one another. If group members start comparing the various translations on a given passage, they find a destabilized biblical text in which modern translations are often widely divergent. There is no incentive for determining what the Bible really says, because laypeople lack the resources for knowing where an English translation has stuck with what the original authors wrote and where the translators have felt free to add and subtract. Even worse, those who *are* sufficiently expert to know these things are privy to something even more alarming: that what a given translation offers to the public as the words of the original biblical text is often not in the original text at all. It is a hoax.

And what about evangelical Bible translators? Don't they agree with the mainstream tradition that the Bible is God's Word? Yes they do, but it often means much less to modern translators than it did to Tyndale and Coverdale and the Genevan translators and the King James committee. In the early tradition, the words that God gave in the original texts were not regarded as expendable.

That is in obvious contrast to what prevails in dynamic equivalent translation. Do the psalmists say "Lord of hosts"? When dynamic equivalence translators assert that this does not communicate much to modern readers and needs to be changed, they contribute to a view of the biblical writers as misjudging readers and "getting it wrong." Does the psalmist say that God's law is better than honey from the honeycomb? Why not render it as "better than red, ripe strawberries" instead?

In place of the Bible as an authoritative Word that cannot be changed, much modern Bible translation is based on the premise that the translators can say it better than the original biblical authors did. This is repeatedly the implied assertion of dynamic equivalent translators. The biblical authors gave us metaphors, but modern readers find that difficult, so modern translators allegedly "improve" the text by removing the metaphors. The Old Testament chronicler claims that various kings slept with their fathers, but modern translators can improve on it. It is no wonder that half a century of dynamic equivalent translations has made the phrase "what the biblical author *was trying to say*" an omnipresent formula in most Christian circles. For the first English translators of the Bible, biblical authors did not *try to say* something; they were masters of communication who said what they meant and what God, in fact, inspired them to write.

SUMMARY

English Bible translations from the era of the Reformation were rooted in the translators' views of the Bible. Starting with the premise that the Bible in its original form was verbally inspired by the Holy Spirit, translators viewed the words of the Hebrew and Greek text as fixed and authoritative. The goal of translation was to bring a reader as close as possible to what the biblical authors actually wrote.

3

PRINCIPLES OF TRANSLATION

When we analyze the traits of a Bible translation, there are two aspects that require attention. One is the *content* of the translation: *what* the translations offer to the Bible-reading public as representing what the original authors wrote (or, in some modern versions, a substitute for what the original authors wrote). The other aspect is the *form* in which biblical authors expressed their thoughts and feelings: the language and style in which the content is packaged. This will be the division of duties between this chapter and the three chapters that follow it.

One more thing needs to be noted. The prefaces to all English Bible translations produced after the middle of the twentieth century provide a full account of the translation philosophy that underlies the translation. The prefaces to translations produced before the rise of dynamic equivalence say little about translation philosophy. The reason is obvious: until the rise of dynamic equivalence, everyone knew what translation philosophy had been followed. This means that when we come to formulate the translation philosophy practiced in the mainstream tradition, we often need to *infer* the translation principles. We have two avenues toward such inference—the actual translations and certain unstated assumptions that we can glimpse when we "read between the lines."

FIDELITY TO THE WORDS OF BIBLICAL AUTHORS

Until the middle of the twentieth century, English Bible translators did not doubt that the purpose of Bible translation was to take a reader as directly as possible to what the biblical authors had written. Why translate if not to convey what the biblical authors had said in *their* language to the minds of English readers in *their* language?

We can see this bias in full form in the translation practices of William Tyndale. Probably the clearest evidence is the words that Tyndale introduced into the English language in his determination to give English readers what the original authors actually wrote. An expert on the origin of English words claims that *The Oxford English Dictionary Based on Historical Principles* (OED) attributes seventeen hundred "first instances" of an English word to William Tyndale and more than five thousand to his associate Miles Coverdale.[1] Some of these words go by the name of Hebraisms—English words coined to match Hebrew words. Examples include *intercession, atonement, scapegoat, Passover*. Other neologisms were simply an attempt to be faithful to the original—formulations such as *lovingkindness, peacemakers, filthy lucre*.

Furthermore, Tyndale believed that there was an inherent correspondence between the Hebrew and Greek languages and the English language. He wrote: "The Greek tongue agreeth more with the English than the Latin. And the properties of the Hebrew tongue agreeth a thousand times more with the English than with the Latin. The manner of speaking is both one; so that in a thousand places thou needest not but to translate it into the English, word for word."[2] To coin new English words in the process of translation might seem to be insignificant, but it is not. It sends a signal that

Tyndale was determined not to swerve from what the authors of the Bible actually wrote.

The same impulse to reproduce in English the words of the original biblical text took an unexpected twist with the Geneva Bible. Anyone familiar with the King James Version (KJV) knows that numerous words and phrases are printed in italics. The practice started with the Geneva Bible. The Genevan translators were so scrupulous to keep the record straight regarding what the original biblical authors actually wrote that they italicized words that the translators added to the original text for the sake of understandability in English. An English Bible requires translators to perform what we today call "smoothing out" the roughness of the Hebrew or Greek text that would result if the original were rendered literally.

Is this the same thing that dynamic equivalent translators do? No, it is not. The italicized words rarely fall into the kind of paraphrase and commentary that are a hallmark of dynamic equivalence. The italics in the Geneva and KJV translations fall into the category of necessary accommodations required by the very process of translation into English. The Genevan and King James translators made the necessary accommodations to English fluency, but that has virtually nothing in common with the liberties taken by dynamic equivalence translators. The earlier translators wanted to spare English readers from any possible confusion in regard to the original text, but they did not think it their prerogative to interpret the text beyond what the biblical authors had provided.

The KJV perpetuated this foundational principle of fidelity to the words of the original text—of making sure that everything in the original text was rendered in an equivalent word or phrase in English. Alister McGrath made a thorough study of the King James Bible and came to the conclusion that the King James translators made every possible effort to do the following:

1. Ensure that every word in the original was rendered by an English equivalent;
2. Make it clear when they added any words to make the sense clearer, or to lead to better English syntax. . . .
3. Follow the basic word order of the original wherever possible.[3]

McGrath adds that "the King James translators seem to have taken the view—which corresponds with the consensus of the day—that an accurate translation is, by and large, a literal and formal translation."[4]

To sum up, the principle I have referred to as fidelity to the words of the biblical authors could equally well be phrased in terms common to the current debate over English Bible translation. Consider these alternate formulas:

- essentially literal translation (but not literal at the cost of intelligibility)
- verbal equivalence (not necessarily "word for word" but rather making sure that everything in the original—but not more than is in the original—finds expression in an equivalent English word or phrase)
- formal equivalence (a theory of translation that believes that the form in which something is expressed is inseparable from the meaning that is expressed, so that an English translation should not lightly dispense with how the original authors expressed their content)
- linguistic conservatism (a general orientation toward conserving the actual words of the original text by finding equivalent words or phrases in English)
- transparency to the original text (removing all obstacles to seeing what the biblical authors wrote and, as part of that,

avoiding an overlay of interpretive commentary or the substitution of something in our own experience for what the
biblical authors wrote)

CLARITY

Bible translators always participate in a balancing act among competing claims. If the urge toward linguistic conservatism is not
balanced by an equal concern for readability in English, the result
is something like the overly literal Revised Version of 1885, which
was almost immediately relegated to the scholar's study and ignored
by the general public.

The need to balance competing interests is highlighted in a document surrounding the first English translations—the Wycliffite.
The Wycliffite Bible exists in two versions. The first was a translation that stayed close to the Latin of the Vulgate. It was not fluent
English. The later translation is much closer to native English
(which, again, was Middle English, not modern English).

The terms in which Wycliffe's associates discussed the matter
have been as misunderstood as Tyndale's plowboy statement. The
statement is this, made by John Purvey in his prologue:

> It should be known that the best way of translating out of Latin
> into English is to translate according to the meaning, and not
> merely according to the words, so that the meaning might be
> as plain, or even more plain, in English as in Latin, while not
> straying any further from the literal translation than is necessary.
> The letter need not always be closely followed in the transla-
> tion, but by all means let the meaning be completely plain, for
> the words of a translation should serve to convey the intended
> meaning, or else the words are useless or false. In translating
> into English, many transformations are necessary in order to
> make the meaning plain.[5]

41

This may sound just like what we find in the prefaces to modern dynamic equivalent translations, but the context rules that out, and so does the actual Wycliffite translation.

The whole preoccupation in Purvey's prologue is how Latinate versus how English a translation should be, not how literal versus how free it should be. As an expert in Wycliffite writings explains, "The debate is not, as a modern critic might suppose, between a close and a free rendering, but between a transposition of Latin into English and a close translation into English word order and vocabulary."[6]

But if Purvey's statement does not plant a flag for loose loyalty to what the biblical authors wrote, it does show a concern for clarity in English. The italicization found in the Geneva and King James versions tells the same story. As already noted, the italicization shows a preoccupation with keeping the record clear regarding what the original authors wrote. But the italicization also sends another message: it shows that the translators were equally concerned to produce a Bible that was fluent in English. The translators *did* add words to smooth out what was abrupt or unclear when the Hebrew and Greek text made its migration to English.

ACCURACY

The criterion of accuracy has implicitly been addressed above in my discussion of the early translators' faithfulness in reproducing the words of the biblical authors. But I need to flag the topic in a separate section of this chapter, because the question of what constitutes accuracy is itself debated on the current scene. Accuracy begins with a correct grasp of what the biblical authors wrote.

In our day we are so accustomed to the premise that English Bible translation must be based on the best original texts of Scripture—Hebrew for the Old Testament and Greek for the New Testament—that we take it for granted. But this is not where English Bible translation began. Wycliffe and his associates started with the Latin Vulgate. Coverdale (who produced the Coverdale Bible, including the Psalter that was used in the Anglican *Book of Common Prayer* right into the twentieth century) did not know Hebrew and Greek.

For the most part, though, the classic tradition of English Bible translation has assumed the original texts as the necessary first leg of the journey toward accuracy of translation. A statement in the preface to the KJV can be taken as a summary of the position. The preface claims that "the *Hebrew* text of the Old Testament, the *Greek* of the New . . . are the two golden pipes, or rather conduits, wherethrough the olive branches empty themselves into the gold." Additionally, the preface asks rhetorically, "If truth [is] to be tried by these tongues, then whence should a translation be made, but out of them?"

The other half of the equation is to find the most accurate word or phrase in English by which to render the words of the original text. In particular, this means finding the current English words that are the lexical equivalent to words in the original text. In practice this means (1) finding words that have the best possible denotative meanings and connotations and (2) avoiding words that have incorrect connotations or shades of meaning. This is rendered all the more difficult because the meanings of words in English are always changing and are relative to specific groups within the broader society. The early translators do not spell this out, but we catch a hint of it in Tyndale's request that if his readers find places where he has "not given the right English word" they inform him of it, adding that members of the body of Christ have a "duty" to amend what is faulty in a translation.[7]

TRANSPARENCY TO THE ORIGINAL TEXT

A translation's transparency became a frequently used concept with the rise of dynamic equivalence in the mid-twentieth century.

The rival translation theories on the scene today have different conceptions of what transparency means. Dynamic equivalence advocates popularized the term, using it to identify their goal of producing a biblical text that was immediately understandable to contemporary English readers. They called such a text transparent, meaning that there is nothing in the text that stands in the way of immediate comprehension.

Advocates of essentially literal translation later adapted the concept of transparency to *their* translation philosophy. They speak of transparency to the original text of the Bible. The goal here is to take the reader directly to the world of the original text. The substitutions for what is in the biblical text that are so dear to dynamic equivalent translators are regarded by essentially literal translators as obstacles to seeing the original text and the world evoked by it.

Translations in the mainstream tradition are transparent in the second sense. How do we know? We know first by the absence of contemporizing touches that remove the biblical text from its ancient setting. A holy kiss remains a holy kiss and does not become "a hearty handshake all the way around." A table full of fatness remains just that and is not translated as "your table with your favorite food." The command to gird up one's loins is kept in view instead of being removed from sight by being rendered "prepare yourself."

When we read translations in the King James tradition, we repeatedly encounter the "otherness" of the biblical world. Translators and readers in this tradition believe that this is exactly what should happen when we read the Bible. The Bible is an ancient book, not a modern one. Except for a few adventuresome touches in Tyndale's translation (such as when he has Paul sail "after the Easter holidays" instead of "after the days of Unleavened Bread" [Acts 20:6]), the main line of English Bible translation until the mid-twentieth century presents a unified front on the desirability of being transparent to the original text.

SUMMARY

My subject in this chapter has been the content of the earliest English Bibles from Wycliffe and Tyndale through the King James—the "what" of the English Bible as distinct from the "how" (to be explored in the next three chapters). As I summarize the subject with a list of what the earliest translators of the English Bible did and refrained from doing, it should be evident that they stood opposed to the practices of some modern translators.

Here are the convictions and procedures of the first English translators of the Bible:

- An English translation must provide an English word or phrase that is the equivalent of every word that appears in the original text.
- A translation must not deceive an English reader in regard to the original text by adding commentary to the original text.
- A translation must not omit anything that is in the original text.
- A translation must not substitute something for what is in the original text.
- The content of the original text must be rendered in clear English.
- Accuracy of translation must be measured by two criteria: faithfulness to the words of the original text and correctness of English vocabulary, grammar, and syntax.
- An English translation must take a reader directly to the world of the original text.
- Conversely, an English translation must not include material—modern substitutes—that deflects a reader from seeing what the biblical authors meant.

4

LANGUAGE AND STYLE

The translation principles that underlie the mainstream tradition are mainly inferred rather than explicitly stated by the translators. For that very reason, most people today are unaware of the degree to which the King James tradition is essentially literal in its orientation, or the way in which translations in this tradition give readers a verbal equivalence to what is in the original text.

However, as I now begin three chapters devoted to features of style, the traits that I cover will be familiar, even for people who might not be able to name the features I discuss. I should also note that in regard to matters of style the King James Version (KJV) can largely be allowed to represent the entire tradition. This is so because the KJV brought to a climax the style that had been evolving through a series of translations. Furthermore, the KJV alone preserved and perpetuated those traits for three centuries.

The stylistic and rhythmic excellence of the King James Bible cannot be fully explained. Something like a benediction fell on the KJV. The best tribute to the uniqueness of the KJV is that the King

James style can be parodied and imitated but never duplicated. I need to clarify that the English Standard Version makes no attempt to duplicate the King James Bible; it transmutes *the qualities* of the KJV into contemporary English.

THREE FALLACIES ABOUT THE STYLE OF THE KJV

Excellent discussions of the language and style of the King James Bible have been in print for a long time. These have kept the public accurately informed about the tradition that is my subject in this book. In recent times, however, enthusiasts for colloquial English Bibles have perpetuated incorrect claims regarding the King James style. Here are three fallacies that should never have received currency:

Fallacy 1: the King James style is a uniformly exalted and ornate style. Three things have given rise to this fallacy. First, for many modern readers the archaic quality of the KJV automatically registers as "exalted and formal." But what strikes modern readers as archaic in the KJV was equally a feature of everyday, person-on-the-street conversation. Second, the avoidance of a colloquial style leads some people to think (again mistakenly) that the style is therefore a high or embellished style. There is something between embellished and colloquial styles. Third, while it is true that the King James Bible contains some very exalted passages, it is an error to think that this is *all* that we find in the KJV.

Fallacy 2: the KJV is more literary than the Bible in its original form. This is only occasionally the case. The claim comes from people with an exaggerated sense of the colloquialism of the original texts of the Bible. The fact that the language of the Greek New Testament was not literary Greek in the manner of Greek tragedies proves little. What counts is what the biblical writers *did* with the words that they used. It is demonstrable that many passages in the Bible are formal and embellished even though the vocabulary

48

was not literary or stylized in its original form. Abraham Lincoln's Gettysburg Address provides a good parallel: its vocabulary is not what makes it eloquent, but rather the ways in which Lincoln molded the words that he used.

Fallacy 3: Tyndale used native Anglo-Saxon words, while the King James translators gravitated toward Latin-derived words. A further dichotomy flows from this fallacy, namely, that Tyndale's words are predominantly monosyllabic, while the words of the KJV are often polysyllabic. Surprisingly, the percentage of Anglo-Saxon words is approximately the same for Tyndale and the KJV—90 percent.[1]

VOCABULARY

The keynote of the King James style is that it possesses a flexibility and variety commensurate with the original texts of the Bible. For that reason, it is hard to come up with the right descriptor by which to name its essence. The vocabulary is predominantly noncolloquial (that is, it is unlike the conversational idiom of teenagers recounting the day's experiences), but that is only to say what it is *not*. On the other hand, the debunkers of the King James tradition are right in claiming that the style of that tradition is not and never was the idiom of the barber shop or small-town newspaper editorial. It is language on its best behavior, not language that is "dressed down."

The adjective *dignified* is perhaps the best umbrella term by which to identify the language preferences of the King James translators. The word *elegant* is also accurate, but in that case we need to dissociate that word from *eloquent* as a "constant" in the King James Bible. The goal of the King James translators was to be answerable to the reverence with which they believed people should approach a sacred text. In their view, the Bible should sound like the Bible, not something as casual as a gossip session in the corner coffee shop.

The quickest way to capture the essence of the classic tradition of English Bible translation is to contrast it to the modern colloquializing tradition. We can compare the following three versions of Acts 8:20:

- "But Peter said unto him, Thy money perish with thee, because thou hast thought that the gift of God may be purchased with money" (KJV).
- "Peter said to him, 'You and your money will both end up in hell if you think you can buy God's gift!'" (CEV).
- "Peter said, 'To hell with your money! And you along with it. Why, that's unthinkable—trying to buy God's gift!'" (MESSAGE).

The King James rendition is predominantly monosyllabic and approximates how an Elizabethan person would have spoken in public. But it is dignified rather than low, and it commands attention and respect because of it. Colloquial translations give us a "dressed down" Bible that people quickly put on a par of importance and respect with the utterances of people who speak like that in everyday life.

COMBINED SIMPLICITY AND MAJESTY

The genius of the style of the classic tradition of English Bible translation is its paradoxical combination of simplicity and majesty. The Bible in its original form has this same dual quality. Literary scholar Northrop Frye wrote that "the simplicity of the AV [KJV] has often been praised, and this too is a quality that belongs to the original. But there are different kinds of simplicity. . . . The simplicity of the Bible is the simplicity of majesty, not of equality, must less of naïveté: its simplicity expressed the voice of authority."[2]

There is a simplicity that diminishes, but there is also a simplicity that enlarges. The King James tradition exemplifies the second kind of simplicity. Here are the verdicts of two scholars on the subject:

- "There is a kind of monosyllabic simplicity and yet majesty about much of the language."[3]
- "But simplicity is not the only quality of the diction of the King James version. It has majesty and stateliness as well."[4]

Contrary to the claims of devotees of colloquial translations, the simple can be a form of beauty and eloquence without being colloquial, and the classic tradition achieves that type of beauty.

Some parts of the King James Bible fall decisively into either a style or an exalted style. The following passage is simplicity in its pure form: "And the servant ran to meet her, and said, Let me, I pray thee, drink a little water of thy pitcher. And she said, Drink, my lord: and she hasted, and let down her pitcher upon her hand, and gave him drink" (Gen. 24:17–18). The King James style is archaic for modern readers, and the event of Abraham's servant meeting Rebekah at the well is momentous, but the narrative style is direct and simple.

When the original text is itself couched in a high style, the King James Bible is similarly exalted. The prologue to John's Gospel echoes a famous hymn to Zeus that the ancient Greeks had sung for centuries by the time John wrote it: "In the beginning was the Word, and the Word was with God, and the Word was God. The same was in the beginning with God. All things were made by him; and without him was not any thing made that was made" (John 1:1–3). Word patterns and other patterns of repetition make this passage poetic and rhetorically embellished.

We can accurately say that the King James Bible as a whole is both simple and grand. Some passages specialize in simplicity, others in eloquence.

But to say only that would be to omit one of the great mysteries of the King James Bible, which is that more often than not the effect of majesty is actually expressed in simple vocabulary and syntax. Here is an example of the kind of passage that is the norm in the King James Bible: "Ask, and it shall be given you; seek, and ye shall find; knock, and it shall be opened unto you. For every one that asketh receiveth; and he that seeketh findeth; and to him that knocketh, it shall be opened" (Luke 11:9–10). The vocabulary is simple, and the sentence elements are brief. On the other side, the passage is a rhetorical tour de force with its elaborate patterns of repetition. It is, in fact, an example of simple form and majestic effect.

APHORISTIC QUALITY

One of the results of the stylistic features that I have noted is that translations in the King James tradition have an aphoristic flair that makes many of their statements almost impossible to forget. An aphorism is a concise, memorable statement of a profound truth. The KJV was the culmination of a century of English Bible translation that tended toward aphoristic greatness.

Experts in the history of the English Bible universally acknowledge the aphoristic greatness of translations in the King James tradition. Here are two representative statements:

- "The language of KJV is beautiful. Right through the sixty-six books of the Bible . . . phrases of lapidary beauty have been deeply admired."[5]
- "The sheer beauty of its phraseology arrests the attention and then lingers in the memory like haunting strains of music."[6]

Modern translations that distance themselves from the King James tradition do not aspire toward aphoristic effect, and they do not achieve it.

What makes a statement memorable and aphoristic? Nearly always it consists of doing something unusual with language. Poetry tends to be more aphoristic than prose, but in the King James Bible aphorisms appear on nearly every page. What I have called the "unusual" element that produces aphoristic effect can be the presence of vivid imagery and metaphor, but often what we call a well-turned phrase gains its effect through special qualities of syntax. Aphorisms are often tight and concise statements, and often they invert normal word order. Whatever the technique, aphoristic writing (with poetry as the prime exhibit) possesses the quality that J. R. R. Tolkien attributed to fantasy, namely, "arresting strangeness."

What are the benefits of writing that possesses an aphoristic flair? Chiefly three: such discourse is beautiful, striking in its impact, and memorable. Producers of modern prosaic Bible translations forfeit the qualities I have named. A Bible translation that sounds like the daily newspaper is given the same level of attention and credence as the daily newspaper.

A single comparison will need to suffice as an illustration. The King James rendition of 1 Timothy 6:6 is oracular: "But godliness with contentment is great gain." This is an aphorism that not only expresses an insight but compels it. Here is how three modern translations manage to drain the verse of its sparkle: "Well, religion does make a person very rich, if he is satisfied with what he has" (GNB). "But godliness *actually* is a means of great gain when accompanied by contentment" (NASB). "And of course religion does yield high dividends, but only to those who are content with what they have" (REB).

EXALTATION AND AFFECTIVE POWER

If aphoristic effect is one of the results of the King James style, another is the exaltation and affective power that are a hallmark of the KJV. Often the effect is achieved by the simplest means imaginable. For example, the presence of the vocative "O" can sweep us upward: "O taste and see that the LORD is good" (Ps. 34:8). Modern translations that remove the "O" lose much of the affective power of the verse: "Taste and see that the LORD is good" (NIV, NLT). Similarly the KJV "O magnify the LORD with me" (Ps. 34:3) has its voltage diminished with such modern renditions as "Glorify the LORD with me" (multiple translations) or "Join me in spreading the news" (MESSAGE).

Small touches add a lot, as the mainstream tradition from William Tyndale onward acknowledged. The interjections *verily, lo,* and *behold* serve as examples. "Verily I say unto you, they have their reward," Tyndale translated Jesus's oracular pronouncement recorded in Matthew 6:2. "And behold there was a great earthquake," we read in Tyndale's account of the resurrection (Matt. 28:2). "And lo I am with you always, even until the end of the world," Tyndale rendered the imposing last verse of Matthew's Gospel.

Vocabulary no doubt plays its part in the affective power of translations in the classic mainstream, but this is very hard to analyze. Here is a typical King James example: "Come unto me, all ye that labour and are heavy laden, and I will give you rest" (Matt. 11:28). The effect is moving and evocative, but the vocabulary is simple. Charles Butterworth attributes the emotional effect of the verse to its content when he writes that anyone who reads the verse "sees before him a doorway of release, and no disquisition on the beauty of the words could make them more acceptable."[7] But the same content in a typical modernizing translation is flat and prosaic: "Come to me, all of you who are tired and have heavy loads, and I will give you rest" (NCV). Or, "Come to me, all you who work hard and who carry heavy burdens and I will refresh you" (Christian Community Bible [popular Catholic translation]).

But of course there are passages where it is demonstrably the high style and complex syntax and embellished rhetorical patterning that make translations in the classic tradition soar. Here is a KJV example: "For I am persuaded, that neither death, nor life, nor angels, nor principalities, nor powers, nor things present, nor things to come, nor height, nor depth, nor any other creature, shall be able to separate us from the love of God, which is in Christ Jesus our Lord" (Rom. 8:38–39).

SUMMARY

The language and style of the classic mainstream tradition of English Bible translation embody the quality of dignity. They are not usually "lofty" or ornate, as people unfamiliar with their archaic flavor are too quick to conclude. The vocabulary and style of the King James tradition are blended and varied. While the style is sometimes exalted, it is more likely to be simple in form and majestic in effect. The King James tradition tends to be aphoristic, beautiful, and memorable, and the effect is one of exaltation and affective splendor.

5

❦

RHYTHM AND ORAL EFFECTS

All that I have attributed to the King James tradition is well attested. Scholars assert these qualities, and they are felt to be true by ordinary people who read the King James Version (KJV). The same is true of the rhythm and oral effects that I discuss in this chapter. I write as a scholar, but the person in the pew knows what I am talking about when I name these features.

THE RENAISSANCE CONTEXT

To understand the superior oral effects of the KJV and its forebears, we need to begin not with the actual translations but with the era that produced them. That era was simultaneously the Reformation and the Renaissance. It was still what historians call an oral culture, though in the process of becoming a print culture.

A good index to the attentiveness of the King James translators to oral effects is provided by John Seldon, who lived approximately contemporaneously with the production of the KJV. Seldon left the following account in his *Table Talk* of how the King James translators proceeded during their final committee meetings. The committee member with responsibility for a given part of the Bible would read the text aloud. If the translators "found any fault, they spoke up; if not, he read on."[1]

We can hardly avoid being surprised by two things in the procedure that Seldon outlines: (1) the conspicuous attentiveness to oral reading and hearing of the Bible during the process of translation and (2) the willingness to allot the extra time that reading the whole Bible aloud would require. Adam Nicolson comments insightfully on the situation: "This is the kingdom of the spoken. . . . The spoken word is the heard word, and what governs acceptability of a particular verse is not only accuracy but euphony."[2] We should note as well that the KJV claimed on its title page that it was "appointed *to be read* in churches" (italics added).

PROSE RHYTHM

Rhythm refers to the flow of language, chiefly discerned in oral reading of a text. The flow of language, in turn, consists primarily of a regularly recurring pattern of syllables, words, and phrases. The wavelike rise and fall of spoken language is the essence of good rhythm, whether in prose or verse. The technical term for this is *cadence*.

The biggest building block in prose is the sentence. We *always* stop at the end of a sentence in both silent and oral reading. But prose rhythm is more governed by phraseology within a sentence. Phraseology is usually highlighted by punctuation marks such as commas and semicolons, but in reading a passage of prose we intuitively make pauses in addition to those indicated by punctuation marks. I will note in passing that the King James Bible of 1611 is overpunctuated by modern standards because the translators wished to aid public reading of the text. The smallest unit of prose rhythm is meter—the arrangement of stressed and unstressed syllables into a pattern of regular recurrence. At this level prose behaves much like poetry.

Smooth flow is the mark of good prose rhythm. Nearly everyone who has written on English Bible translation agrees that the prose rhythm of the King James Bible is matchless. Almost any prose passage from the King James Bible will validate the accolades. Here is the King James rhythm in a narrative passage (Mark 4:36–39, with original punctuation retained):

> And when they had sent away the multitude, they took him, even as he was in the ship, and there were also with him other little ships. And there arose a great storm of wind, and the waves beat into the ship, so that it was now full. And he was in the hinder part of the ship asleep on a pillow: and they awake him, and say unto him, Master, carest thou not, that we perish? And he arose, and rebuked the wind, and said unto the sea, Peace, be still: and the wind ceased, and there was a great calm.

This passage is "scripted" for oral reading. The retention of the Greek *kai*, translated as a coordinating conjunction *and*, is fully evident and keeps the momentum flowing. The passage is a seamless rhythmic progression.

Prose rhythm is as important to the discourse sections of the King James Bible as it is in the narrative sections. Here is an excerpt from the set-piece of exalted King James prose, the epithalamion in praise of love in 1 Corinthians 13: "And though I bestow all my goods to feed the poor, and though I give my body to be burned, and have not charity, it profiteth me nothing. Charity suffereth long, and is kind; charity envieth not; charity vaunteth not itself, is not puffed up. . . ; beareth all things, believeth all things, hopeth all things, endureth all things" (vv. 3–4, 7). The passage flows in a wavelike cadence built out of the rise and fall of sound. The passage also shows that the *eth* endings of the inflected verbs constitutes an unaccented syllable that plays a key role in keeping the rhythm flowing. Robbed of these unaccented endings, modern translations often bump along in staccato fashion: "always protects, always trusts, always hopes, always perseveres" (NIV).

THE COORDINATING CONJUNCTION *AND*

We cannot read very far in the King James Bible without perceiving a more-than-ordinary number of occurrences of the coordinating conjunction *and*: "And Abram went up out of Egypt. . . . And Abram was very rich in cattle, in silver, and in gold. And he went on his journeys. . . . : and there Abram called on the name of the LORD" (Gen. 13:1–4). This stylistic trait began with William Tyndale: "And when even was come, his disciples went unto the sea and entered into a ship, and went over the sea unto Capernaum. And anon it was dark, and Jesus was not come to them. And the sea arose with a great wind that blew" (John 6:16–18).

Modern readers naturally wonder what is going on. The reason for the prevalence is actually simple. William Tyndale and his heirs were committed to producing an essentially literal translation. A stylistic distinctive of Old Testament Hebrew is the connecting word *waw*. The counterpart in the Greek New Testament is *kai*. The normal way of rendering these words in English is *and*.

I could hardly believe my ears when a British pastor cited this as evidence that the English Standard Version (ESV) was not as readable as desirable. And Eugene Nida had the nerve to call this feature of the Bible in its original and translated forms "childish."[3] I do not share those opinions.

The conjunction *and* not only provides a tremendous sense of continuity, but it also contributes to the smooth flow of meter (which is why I discuss the matter in a chapter on rhythm and oral effects). Here is a typical example from the KJV: "And I will set a sign among them, and I will send those that escape of them unto the nations . . . and they shall declare my glory among the Gentiles. And they shall bring all your brethren for an offering unto the LORD" (Isa. 66:19–20). The connective *and* makes the passage more readable than it would otherwise be.

POETIC RHYTHM

At least a third of the Bible comes to us in the form of verse and poetry. The subject of poetic rhythm in an English translation is obviously a major issue, not a minor one. Here, too, the King James tradition proves its mettle.

Lane Cooper, in a monograph titled *Certain Rhythms in the English Bible*, shows how certain passages of poetry in the KJV fall into the ordinary categories of rhythm found in English poetry.[4] Thus the second verse of Psalm 73 falls into regular iambic feet (consisting of an unaccented syllable followed by an accented syllable): "But AS for ME, my FEET were ALmost GONE; my STEPS had WELL nigh SLIPPED." Verses 3 and 6 of Psalm 23 are predominantly anapestic (two unaccented syllables followed by an accented one, to make a poetic foot consisting of three syllables): "he reSTOReth my SOUL"; "I [unaccented] will DWELL in the HOUSE of the LORD for EVer."

Good poetic rhythm came naturally to the King James translators because they lived in an oral culture in which the Bible was read daily in religious settings. The language they used had the additional rhythmic benefit of unaccented inflected verb endings: "whatsoEVer he DOeth shall PROSper" (Ps. 1:3); "he CASTeth FORTH his ICE like MORsels" (Ps. 147:17).

When modern translators make a conscious break with the King James tradition, the deficiency in rhythm shows itself repeatedly. As an example, we can compare the following two versions of Psalm 24:1:

> The EARTH is the LORD'S, and the FULness thereOF;
> The WORLD, and THEY that DWELL thereIN.
>
> The EARTH is the LORD's and ALL that is IN IT,
> the WORLD, and ALL who DWELL IN IT.

I chose this as an example of how some of the archaic constructions of the KJV (in this case the words *thereof* and *therein*) are a great aid to smooth rhythm. Robbed of those resources, the second rendition ends the lines in a jolting and staccato manner.

SUMMARY

To bring this chapter into focus, I can do no better than allow a scholar to speak for me: "The King James men had ears. As Jacobeans they were more sensitive to speech rhythms and more practiced in them, far better trained in rhetoric and respectful of it, than their modern successors."[5] But I need to guard against a misconception that might creep in, namely, that a modern translation cannot be rhythmically excellent. The ESV reaps the harvest of excellence represented by the King James tradition by following the cadence of the KJV as much as modern English usage allows.

6

A LITERARY BIBLE

The Bible in its original form is a literary anthology. By this I mean not only that it consists of literary genres such as narrative, poetry, vision, and epistle, but also that the style of writing is literary. While it is partly the case that even the most colloquial and nonliteral of English translations cannot help but preserve the genres of the original, that turns out to be less true than we might initially think (as will be evident when I discuss poetry, below).

The foundational premise of literature is that it does things with language that ordinary discourse does not do. Even modern realistic literature is far more carefully crafted and arranged than everyday speech is. This means that a translation that aims to sound like a church newsletter or conversation at the bus stop has headed in a nonliterary direction before the translation process even begins. The Tyndale–King James tradition did not take that turn.

THE VERDICT OF LITERARY SCHOLARS

Before I look at the literary properties of the King James Version (which was the culmination of the preceding tradition), I want to take a brief excursion into what literary scholars say about English

Bible translations. I do not know of any literary scholar or author who uses anything other than the King James Version (KJV) or a modern successor as the Bible of choice. In chapter 11 of my book *The Legacy of the King James Bible,* I cite numerous statements from literary figures who extol the literary superiority of the KJV. Although this does not demonstrate *how* the King James tradition is literary in nature, it serves as a preliminary signpost *that* the classic tradition of English Bible translation is a literary tradition.

It might seem unlikely that William Tyndale and the King James translators would produce a literary Bible. The main goal of these translators was to produce an accurate translation so that readers might know the mind of God and achieve the salvation of their souls. Literary excellence was presumably not in their minds. After all, they were not literary scholars but specialists in Hebrew and Greek.

But this should not lead us to prejudge anything about literary *effect* (as distinct from the *aim* of the translators). Alister McGrath hits the nail on the head when he writes as follows: "Paradoxically, the king's translators achieved literary distinction precisely because they were not deliberately pursuing it. Aiming at truth, they achieved what later generations recognized as beauty and elegance. . . . Elegance was achieved by accident, rather than design." McGrath also tucks in the idea that the literary achievement of the King James translators was "a most happy accident of history."[1]

McGrath's appeal to history needs to be elaborated. If we know enough about Renaissance education and culture, it is not so surprising that the biblical scholars who produced the KJV gave us a literary Bible. The Renaissance was the great age of humanism. The arts were cultivated with zest. Beauty was esteemed. The English language was at a moment of great energy and expansiveness. Eloquence and rhetorical mastery were the very goal of Renaissance education.[2]

There is an additional factor as well. The Bible in its original form is a thoroughly literary book. The Tyndale–King James tradition believed in essentially literal translation. It is no surprise that careful adherence to the original text produces a literary translation. Literary author Reynolds Price has written: "The power and memorability of the King James is an almost automatic result of its loyal adherence to principles of literalness and the avoidance of paraphrase."[3]

CONCRETENESS AND VIVIDNESS OF LANGUAGE

The motto of writing teachers is that the task of literature is to show rather than tell—to embody and incarnate rather than spell out in a series of propositions. This immediately activates a further criterion: literary language is concrete rather than abstract.

A notable feature of dynamic equivalent translations is the impulse to Spell It Out, and this often means abandoning concretion in favor of abstraction. This is not surprising. The impulse behind dynamic equivalence is to add commentary and explanation to the biblical text. Such commentary is almost always abstract.

By contrast, the tradition stemming from Tyndale sticks with the concreteness of the original. The language of the Hebrew Old Testament, in particular, is marked by concrete vocabulary. Here are three scholarly comments that drive the point home:

- "Nearly every word presents a concrete meaning, clearly visible even through a figurative use. . . . Everywhere we are face to face with motion, activity, life."[4]
- "That is the natural method of the Hebrew language—concrete, vivid, never abstract, simple in its phrasing. The King James translators are exceedingly loyal to that original."[5]
- "In Hebrew . . . the vocabulary was consciously pictorial and concrete in its character. . . . The writers of the Old Testament—and to a less degree those of the New as well—thought and felt and spoke in images. . . . The Biblical

vocabulary is compact of the primal stuff of our universal humanity—of its universal emotional, sensory experiences."[6]

The KJV and its forebears preserve such concreteness in all of the biblical genres.

Poetry is the clearest example. There is no point at which the KJV abandons the concrete vocabulary of the original, as in the following pictorial rehearsal of what the worshiper remembers from his pilgrimage to the temple: "Yea, the sparrow hath found an house, and the swallow a nest for herself, where she may lay her young, even thine altars, O LORD of hosts, my King, and my God" (Ps. 84:3).

Prose narrative has the same tangible quality. The moment of Ehud's assassination of Eglon comes alive in vivid detail when we read about it thus: "And Ehud put forth his left hand, and took the dagger from his right thigh, and thrust it into his belly: And the haft also went in after the blade; and the fat closed upon the blade, so that he could not draw the dagger out of his belly; and the dirt came out" (Judg. 3:21–22).

We are so accustomed to having the New Testament epistles transmuted into theological abstraction that we have come to think of them as primarily propositional. But they are not that way in the original. Here is an example from Tyndale's New Testament: "Even unto this day we hunger and thirst, and are naked, and are buffeted with fists, and have no certain dwelling place, and labor working with our own hands" (Paul's autobiographical sketch in 1 Cor. 4:11–12).

RETAINING FIGURATIVE LANGUAGE

I know that some of my readers will be thinking that *of course* English Bibles retain the concrete vividness of the Bible's imagery. That is largely but not totally true for what I call the "straight image" as discussed in the preceding paragraphs. But the picture changes drastically when we come to figurative language. Figures of speech are concrete images first of all, and only after grasping the image are we in a position to carry over the meaning from "level A" to "level B." Translations that are based on the premise that modern readers cannot perform that task of comparison often remove the image (level A) and replace it with an interpretation (level B). For example, in the portrait of aging that the writer of Ecclesiastes gives us in the last chapter of the book, trembling arms are rendered metaphorically as "the keepers of the house tremble" (12:3, KJV). A dynamic equivalent translation removes the metaphor in favor of an abstraction: "your body will grow feeble" (CEV).

The King James tradition does not flinch with figurative language. It puts into English what the original text says, even in the few instances where the meaning is baffling. But usually the meaning is not baffling, and at this point we need to be aware that poetry *precedes* prose in the history of most cultures. Poetry is not an unnatural way of speaking and thinking.

There are two ways in which many modern translations show their nervousness about figurative language. One is by adding commentary to explain what a figure of speech means. The other is to omit the figure of speech completely, and that usually means replacing an image with an abstraction. The KJV renders Psalm 16:6 as it is in the original: "The lines are fallen unto me in pleasant places; yea, I have a goodly heritage." This is an allusion to the dividing of the land when the Israelites entered Canaan.

Dynamic equivalent translators tend to distrust figurative language (though not to the same degree across the board). The following translations add commentary to Psalm 16:6, not trusting the poetic statement to achieve its end by poetic means (I have added italics to accentuate what is added to the original): "the *boundary* lines have fallen for me in pleasant places" (NIV, NRSV); "*the land you have given me* is a pleasant *land*" (NLT). The more drastic maneuver of dropping the metaphor and substituting an abstraction is represented by the following translations: "You make my life pleasant" (CEV); "How wonderful are your gifts to me; // how good they are!" (GNB).

There is no need to give further examples. The Tyndale–King James tradition retains figurative language. Dynamic equivalent translations often remove it.

VARIETY OF GENRE AND AUTHORIAL IMPRINT

In its external format, the Bible is a literary anthology. Even the word *Bible*—"little books"—signals this. What do we expect in an anthology of literature? A literary anthology—I think of *The Norton Anthology of English Literature*—answers the question: we expect a variety of authors, genres, and styles. We might think that *any* English translation of the Bible will preserve the variety that the Bible in its original form possesses, but the matter is not quite that simple. The variety that is native to the Bible in the original text can be neutralized by the advent of something called a target audience.

A target audience is the readership toward which the translators slant their translation. For example, if a committee makes a decision not to exceed a sixth-grade level of vocabulary and syntax, sixth graders become the standard that guides the translation committee in its vocabulary and syntax for its translation. Or the target audience might be women or people ignorant of Christian theology or people who understand a contemporary and colloquial idiom only. In fact, these are the preferred target audiences of many modern translations (as their prefaces sometimes state).

The inevitable result of such a translation is that everything in the original gets flattened out to the linguistic and theological abilities of the target audience. The style of the Bible becomes a uniform style. If an audience is assumed to be incapable of understanding poetry, poetry is made to sound like prose. If the audience is assumed to have had little or no previous or current contact with the Bible, theological vocabulary is removed. And so forth.

The Tyndale–King James tradition has a built-in curb against such neutralizing. By remaining faithful to the very words that the biblical authors wrote, essentially literal translations inevitably reproduce the variety of subject matter, style, and tone of the Bible.

"ARRESTING STRANGENESS"

When we start to peruse a literary anthology such as *The Norton Anthology of English Literature*, we are dazzled with the variety—variety of time period, of author, of genre, of style, of subject matter. Despite this variety, however, on every page we find one thing that is constant: the writing advertises its literary quality by being something beyond everyday expository discourse. We know that a text is literary if it has the quality that J. R. R. Tolkien attributed to fantasy—"arresting strangeness."[7] This quality becomes intensified when the literature comes to us from the remote past.

One of the great strengths of the King James tradition of English Bible translation is the degree to which the writing possesses the literary quality of being extraordinary—words and syntax that are different from and better than the discourse at the grocery store. Conversely, modern translations that pride themselves on sounding like the newspaper show their literary deficiency most obviously at this very point. The daily newspaper and everyday conversation do not use language in a literary manner.

The commitment to treat the Bible as representing an extraordinary use of language began with William Tyndale. We do not need to go to exalted discourses such as the Sermon on the Mount or Paul's address to the Areopagus to find examples; all we need to do is dip randomly into a narrative text from Tyndale's Gospels: "Then he entered into a ship and passed over and came into his own city. And lo, they brought to him a man sick of the palsy, lying in his bed. And when Jesus saw the faith of them, he said to the sick of the palsy: son, be of good cheer, thy sins be forgiven thee. And behold certain of the scribes said in themselves, this man blasphemeth" (Matt. 9:1–3). This is not how the plowboy of Tyndale's day talked in the local pub. The words are relatively simple, but numerous features of the passage make it literary rather than ordinary.

This will be even clearer if we compare Tyndale's version with a modern colloquial version: "Jesus got into a boat and crossed back over to the town where he lived. Some people soon brought to him a crippled man lying on a mat. When Jesus saw how much faith they had, he said to the crippled man, 'My friend, don't worry! Your sins are forgiven.' Some teachers of the Law of Moses said to themselves, 'Jesus must think he is God!' (CEV). Even David Daniell, who wishes to push William Tyndale in a colloquial direction, concedes that Tyndale "translated into a register just above common speech."[8]

There is no need to belabor the point. The Tyndale–King James tradition produced Bibles that rise to a literary level and are demonstrably different from the chatting that goes on in the church narthex.

SUMMARY

The Bible is a literary book. Translations that follow the contours of the original text do a good job of capturing the literary qualities of the Bible. But it is possible to override the literary nature of the Bible by superimposing a commitment to reduce everything to a predetermined level (such as a sixth-grade reading level or the norm of everyday conversational prose). The classic mainstream preserves the literary quality of the Bible. These translations make a sacred text *sound* like a sacred text. They have the literary quality of arresting difference from the ordinary. A literary scholar correctly said that the KJV has the "power of enchantment in a most remarkable degree."[9]

7

A UNIFIED TRADITION

Six English Bible translations from the sixteenth century reached their culminiation in the King James Version (KJV) of 1611 saw the publication of seven English Bible translations. When we look at the list of these translations, it is easy to look at it through the lens of our moment in history and think of these translations as rivals, as different from one another as possible. We need help in reconstructing what actually happened in this regard. The purpose of the current chapter is to show the degree to which the translations from Tyndale through the KJV are really a single (even coordinated) project whose goal was to produce the best English Bible possible. There has never been a better orchestrated project involving so many different Bible scholars spanning so many decades.

EXPLODING A MYTH

Before we can get an accurate picture of the unified achievement of sixteenth-century English Bible translation, we need to lay to rest a myth that has emerged in recent years with the rise of colloquial translations. For advocates of such translations, the King James

Bible is the great enemy because it is sonorous (a favorite term of denigration among advocates of informal-language translations), elegant, smooth-flowing, and beautiful. That is an honest disagreement with the stylistic choices of the King James translators.

But a further claim has entered the picture that is false. The attempt is made to drive a wedge between William Tyndale and the King James translators. Tyndale's translation is touted as a racy, bold, colloquial translation that the King James translators spoiled by introducing something brand new into the mix. Here is an example of the charge: "The King James translators used Tyndale's text as their baseline. . . . But what they did with that plagiarized text amounted to a violation of it—they put lace cuffs on Tyndale's sentences. . . . They skillfully and thoroughly shifted the tone of the language from the roughness of Tyndale's plowboy to the smooth speech of the royal court."[1]

Everything in that statement by Eugene Peterson is incorrect. As we will see, Tyndale would not even understand the charge of plagiarism in this context. In fact, by Peterson's logic, Tyndale's famous plowboy statement was plagiarized from Erasmus![2] Furthermore, I have already shown that Tyndale's "plowboy" statement was not a comment on Tyndale's preferred English style in Bible translation but rather a comment on how broadly he wished English people to know the Bible.

Regarding the claim that the King James translators suddenly altered Tyndale's work, here are three preliminary considerations:

- Tyndale was a pioneer whose main goal was to get the content of the Bible before his countrymen in their native language. He did not have leisure to think about nuances of English style.
- Tyndale himself implicitly acknowledged that his first translation needed improvement when he gave priority to revising

his New Testament (published 1534) instead of working full time on the Old Testament. In fact, he made more than five thousand revisions to his 1526 New Testament.

- Other translators began refining Tyndale's translation while he himself was still alive, as represented by the work of two of his former associates—Miles Coverdale (whose complete Bible was published a year before Tyndale's death) and John Rogers (whose translation called Matthew's Bible was published a year after Tyndale's death). As C. L. Wrenn correctly states, "Many of Tyndale's colloquialisms were replaced . . . by forms of more dignity and depth."[3]

The King James translators did not reverse anything but instead wrote the climactic chapter of a long story of an evolving English Bible.

But we are not left with inferences only. In the preface to his New Testament, Tyndale himself offers an apology for the style of his pioneering effort and signals a degree of unease about it. Tyndale expresses the wish

> that the rudeness of the work now at the first time offend not [my readers], but that they consider how that I had no man to [imitate], neither was [helped] with English of any that had interpreted the same or such like thing in the scripture before time. . . . Many things are lacking, which necessarily are required. Count it as a thing not having his full shape, but as it were born afore his time, even as a thing begun rather than finished.[4]

It is thus no discredit to Tyndale to agree with Adam Nicolson's statement that "Tyndale was working alone, in extraordinary isolation. His only audience was himself. And surely as a result there is a slightly bumpy, stripped straightforwardness about his matter and his rhythm. . . . [The words of the KJV] are clarified where Tyndale's are clotted; they are memorable where Tyndale stumbles over his grammar; the Jacobean choice of word is more authoritative."[5]

The irony of claims by scholars such as David Daniell (who accuses the King James translators of Latinizing Tyndale's translation) and Eugene Peterson (who claims that the King James translators put lace cuffs on Tyndale) is that the five thousand revisions that Tyndale himself made to his original translation are of exactly the same type as the small touches that the King James translators introduced. For example, Tyndale changed "O ye endued with little faith" to "O ye of little faith." He reversed the word order from "behold here is a greater than Solomon" to "and behold a greater than Solomon is here."

THE RENAISSANCE VIEW OF COMMUNAL SCHOLARSHIP

Eugene Peterson's use of the term *plagiarized text* for the King James translators' incorporation of Tyndale should be labeled for what it is—frivolous and irresponsible. In no field, but in Bible translation least of all, did our forebears of the Middle Ages and Renaissance regard scholarly insight as individual property. Instead they regarded it as a shared possession.

Alister McGrath has written with particular excellence on this subject. His starting point is the King James translators. "They stood in a long line of translators," writes McGrath, "and were conscious that their task would be influenced . . . by the English translations already in circulation." McGrath's fuller analysis is as follows: "Lying behind this is an attitude toward wisdom that has largely been lost in the modern period. Writers of the Renaissance were conscious of standing with a stream of cultural and intellectual achievement, from which they benefited and to which they were called to contribute. The wisdom of the past was to be appreciated in the present." McGrath concludes that "the King James Bible can be seen as one of the most outstanding representatives of this corporate approach to cultural advance and the enterprise of gaining wisdom."[6]

SIXTEENTH-CENTURY BIBLE TRANSLATION AS A JOINT PROJECT

With the foregoing context in place, we can understand clearly what was happening in England during the sixteenth century, culminating in the King James Version of 1611. The most helpful statement appears in the preface to the KJV, where the translators state the following: "Truly (good Christian Reader) we never thought from the beginning, that we should need to make a new Translation, nor yet to make of a bad one a good one . . . but to make a good one better, or out of many good ones, one principal good one, not to be excepted against."

This statement tells us a great deal. All translations in the sixteenth century subsequent to Tyndale started with an existing English Bible as their working text. For example, the King James translators were given a mandate to revise the Bishops' Bible of 1568. Second, the King James preface goes out of its way to commend the preceding translations (in contrast to the prevailing spirit today, where one translation committee views another as a rival). Third, the stated goal of producing a culminating "best of the best" translation shows the degree to which sixteenth-century translators viewed the enterprise as an ongoing, multicommittee process.

A NATURAL EVOLUTION

The process of refinement from Tyndale to the KJV has received excellent treatment by nearly a century of published scholarship on the subject. One of the best insights is the following, by John

Livingston Lowes in his classic essay "The Noblest Monument of English Prose": the Authorized Version "represents a slow, almost impersonal evolution. For it is, in reality, itself a revision, resting upon earlier versions, and these, in turn, depend in varying degrees upon each other, so that through the gradual exercise of something which approaches natural selection, there has come about, in both diction and phraseology, a true survival of the fittest. . . . The long process of version upon version served (to use Dante's phrase) as 'a sieve for noble words.'"[7]

One way to see this is to collect some famous words and phrases that various translations added to the process of refinement that culminated in the KJV. Here are examples:

- Tyndale: *be not weary in well doing; my brother's keeper; the salt of the earth; the signs of the times; a law unto themselves; the spirit is willing, but the flesh is weak; fight the good fight; with God all things are possible; the patience of Job; an eye for an eye; O ye of little faith; he went out . . . and wept bitterly; give us this day our daily bread; in him we live and move and have our being*
- Coverdale*: the valley of the shadow of death; thou anointest my head with oil; baptized into his death; tender mercies; loving-kindness; respect of persons; even, neither,* and *yea* (to introduce a Hebrew parallelism)
- Geneva: *smite them hip and thigh; vanity of vanities; my cup runneth over; except a man be born again; comfort ye, comfort ye my people; Solomon in all his glory; my beloved Son in whom I am well pleased*
- Bishops' Bible: blessed are they that *have been persecuted* for righteousness' sake; *the place of a skull;* made *in the likeness* of men; *joint heirs* with Christ; love *worketh no ill* to his neighbor; *a more excellent* sacrifice; the *power* of his resurrection

76

- KJV: *how are the mighty fallen; a still small voice; the root of the matter; beat their swords into plowshares; a thorn in the flesh*

The fact that all of these formulations appear in the culminating KJV proves my point that sixteenth-century English Bible translation was a unified achievement.

An alternate way to show the process of refinement is to compare different versions in chronological order in their handling of a common passage. Here are three successive versions of John 15:12–13, reprinted in original spelling:

- Tyndale: "Thys ys my commaundement, that ye love togedder as I have loved you. Gretter love then this hath no man, then that a man bestowed his lyfe for his frendes."
- Geneva: "This is my commandement, that ye loue one another, as I haue loued you. Greater loue then this hathe no man, when any man bestoweth his life for his friends."
- KJV: "This is my Commaundement, that ye loue one another, as I have loued you. Greater loue hath no man then this, that a man lay downe his life for his friends."

Each successive translation improves on its predecessor.

For a more thorough illustration, we can add more translations to the pool. The following are successive versions of a portion of Matthew 6:34:

- Tyndale: "For the daye present hath ever ynough of his awne trouble."
- Coverdale: "Every daye hath ynough of his owne travayll."
- Great Bible: "Sufficient unto the daye is the travayle therof."
- Geneva: "The day hathe ynough with his owne grief."
- KJV: "Sufficient unto the day is the evil thereof."

William Tyndale deserves all the credit that has been heaped on him during the past two decades. However, nothing is gained by denying that he is sometimes in need of refinement, as he himself acknowledged.

SUMMARY

We can trust the verdicts of earlier scholars who wrote on sixteenth-century Bible translation before advocates of colloquial translations and paraphrases made misleading claims about William Tyndale. I offer three commendations:

- Some of the KJV "adjustments had the Midas touch." And: "In a cumulative way, all the virtues of the various translations which preceded it were gathered up."[8]
- The KJV "was no sudden miracle but rather the harvesting or refining of the previous century's experience of translating the Bible into English."[9]
- "The King James version shows a superb faculty of selection and combination, a sure instinct for betterment."[10]

PART TWO

Modern Bible Translation in Its Context

8

MODERN TRANSLATION
AT THE CROSSROADS

As the centuries unfolded, the King James Version (KJV) naturally began to show its age. Attempts were made to dethrone it, but none of them succeeded until the middle of the twentieth century. A crucial difference characterizes earlier attempts (the most notable of which was the Revised Version of 1885) and modern dynamic equivalent translations. Until the middle of the twentieth century, new translation efforts did not reject the essentially literal philosophy of the classic mainstream tradition. To a slightly lesser degree, adherence to the language and style of the King James tradition remained dominant.

When dynamic equivalence arose, translators suddenly faced a need to choose between rival philosophies of translation and style. My purpose in this chapter is to delineate how modern translations have lined up in their stance toward the classic mainstream tradition.

THE CONTEXT

Until the middle of the twentieth century, the classic mainstream of English Bible translation, as codified by the KJV, was the only viable tradition on the landscape. It was what all English-speaking people meant when they spoke of "the Bible." In a way that now strikes us as quaintly simple and even naïve, authors of Bible commentaries did not think it necessary to identify what English translation they were using. Everyone knew what that translation was. When I read some of the Bible-as-literature books from the first half of the twentieth century, it is as though the authors equated the King James Bible with the Bible in its original form.

Everything changed with the advent of Eugene Nida and dynamic equivalence. The Revised Standard Version of 1952 was the last major English Bible whose preface does not align the translation on one side of a great divide. (The preface does, however, articulate where the translators stood on the issues.) Today translators either align themselves with the classic mainstream tradition or distance themselves from it.

PERPETUATING THE GREAT TRADITION

I will begin with the three modern translations that align themselves with the Tyndale–King James tradition. These translations are the Revised Standard Version (RSV), the New King James Version (NKJV), and the English Standard Version (ESV). The prefaces to these translations signal where the translators stood on the translation debate, and they delineate three things in particular.

First, the prefaces to these translations explicitly state that they belong to the King James tradition. After internal debate, the RSV committee decided to "stay as close to the Tyndale–King James tradition" as it could while maintaining accuracy to the original texts and fluency in English. The preface to the NKJV claims that the translators perceived their work "as a continuation of the labors of the earlier translators" (meaning the tradition of Tyndale and the KJV). And the preface to the ESV asserts that the translation "stands in the classic mainstream of English Bible translations."

A second way in which these three translations tip their hands in the direction of the mainstream tradition is the stated commitment to an essentially literal philosophy of translation. The preface to the RSV does not assert this, but in a related book one of the translators writes that the translator "is charged to tell as accurately as he can in his own language precisely what the original says. . . . The Bible translator is not an expositor."[1] The preface to the NKJV records the committee's rejection of dynamic equivalence, because it "commonly results in paraphrasing where a more literal rendering is needed." The preface to the ESV endorses " 'word-for-word' correspondence."

Third, all three translations wish to be identified with the stylistic excellence of the matchless KJV. The RSV committee claims that its words are "enduring words that are worthy to stand in the great Tyndale–King James tradition." The preface to the NKJV names multiple literary qualities that it carried over from the 1611 Authorized Version. And the ESV preface correctly claims that the translation "carries forward classic translation principles in its literary style."

REJECTION OF THE KING JAMES TRADITION

When we move from the prefaces just discussed to the prefaces of dynamic equivalent translations, we enter a completely different world. What we find there is partly the "cold-shoulder treatment," and partly an outright repudiation of the mainstream tradition. I want to begin, not with the prefaces to these translations, but with statements by individual translators.

83

All that we need to know about the rejection of the King James lineage by dynamic equivalent translators can be found in kernel form in an interview of the founding father of dynamic equivalence, Eugene Nida, who claims that he has "not met one English-speaking person who can tell me what [the petition in the Lord's Prayer *Hallowed be thy name*] means." Bible readers who have used a traditional translation like the KJV have "grown up worshiping words more than worshiping God." And: "As long as all people had the King James Version" says Nida, "they didn't think."[2]

Members of the translation committee of the New International Version (NIV) are equally hostile. Calvin Linton could have articulated the stylistic philosophy of the NIV without denigrating the KJV, but he chose to assert that a modern translation needs "not to be intimidated by the King James Version peering over its shoulder."[3] Edwin H. Palmer, committee member of the NIV, made the hostile comment: "Do not give them a loaf of bread, covered with an inedible, impenetrable crust, fossilized by three and half centuries."[4]

In a class by itself is Eugene Peterson's vendetta against the KJV. Peterson claims that the King James translators "desecrated [language] upward" by producing a fluent and beautiful translation. Peterson paints a picture, totally inaccurate, of the translators doing their work "in the sumptuous furnishings of the great universities and the royal court." It is "a great irony" to Peterson that the KJV is "the Bible of choice for so many people, across the years and today." As a final sneer, Peterson suggests that "it is not known if they read it or not."[5] (My own guess is that rank-and-file KJV users know the Bible better than their counterparts who use modernizing translations.)

The sources that I have quoted are not simply the voice of disagreement with the translation philosophy and practices of the mainstream translators. It is the voice of disrespect. I will note in passing that the King James Bible is by far the most influential Christian book in the history of English-speaking cultures.

If we turn to the prefaces of dynamic equivalent translations, there is little to adduce as evidence. We are faced with an argument from silence: one will look in vain for any statement linking the translation with the classic mainstream tradition. One gets the impression that the translators wish that the mainstream from Tyndale through the ESV did not exist.

Summary

The whole history of English Bible translations from Wycliffite beginnings through the RSV was a relatively simple story of a single dominant way of translating the Bible. The keynotes of that tradition were commitment to translate the words of the original into English (an "essentially literal" philosophy) and dignity of style (avoidance of colloquialism). For the past half century, all translation committees have found ways to align themselves with or repudiate the classic mainstream tradition.

9

WHAT REVIEWERS SAY ABOUT
MODERNIZING TRANSLATIONS

In the other chapters of this book, I advance my own viewpoints and arguments. In this chapter I will let others state the
case for an essentially literal and literarily excellent English
Bible. The reviewers to whom I refer in the title of this chapter
are reviewers who are sympathetic with the classic tradition of
English Bible translation. I do not mean to imply that dynamic
equivalent and colloquial translations do not also have sympathetic reviewers.

Most of the reviewers quoted in this chapter were responding
to the New English Bible (NEB), published in its entirety in 1970.
But this is almost an irrelevance. What they object to in principle
is modernizing translations—translations that are couched in the
language of informal spoken discourse and that accept the premise
of dynamic equivalence that what the biblical authors actually wrote
can be changed by means of paraphrase, omission, substitution,
and the addition of commentary. The reviewers say exactly what I

want said, but they do so with absolutely no recourse to the English Standard Version (ESV), the New International Version (NIV), or any other currently prominent translation (with the exception of the King James Version [KJV]).

A Preview of the Issues

Several layers of protest can be discerned in the objections of the reviewers to modernizing translations. At one level, the departure from the KJV offended the sensibilities of the reviewers. The rejection of modernizing was a matter of taste and preference for the familiar. Taste is a valid criterion by which to assess an English Bible, but of course people's tastes do not uniformly agree with those of the reviewers whom I survey.

As the reviewers become more analytic and objective in approach, underlying issues, and not just taste, become important. The main concern of the reviewers is with language and style, and not the accuracy with which a translation has rendered the original Hebrew and Greek. But it is important to understand that an English translation consists ultimately of words. It is not frivolous, therefore, to say a given translation is best because its words and language are the best.

The reviewers all begin with the premise that the KJV represents the standard of what we want in an English Bible. Their objections to modernizing are a litany of things that they believe have been lost when compared with the King James tradition. I have allowed that approach to form my template for this chapter, and I have accordingly phrased my headings as *things that are lost* when translators reject the principles of the classic mainstream tradition. I leave it to my readers to draw the unstated conclusion that devotees of translations such as the New King James Bible (NKJV) and the ESV feel exactly the same way about dynamic equivalence and colloquial translations.

LOSS OF LANGUAGE

It is well established that in the sixteenth century English Bible translation contributed immensely to the English language. In fact, the English Bible was a major shaper of the English language as it has existed for four hundred years. I noted earlier that the *Oxford English Dictionary* ascribes nearly seven thousand "first instances" of English words to William Tyndale and his assistant Miles Coverdale.[1] This rich lexical heritage is the context for the anger that reviewers voice over the diminishment of language in modern translations that abandon the King James tradition. "They have done wrong to our language," writes a reviewer, "by not stretching it at any point; the richest of all the world's languages, treated as post-office savings."[2]

LOSS OF THE STYLISTIC VARIETY OF THE ORIGINAL

When translators see it as their task to reproduce in English the actual words of biblical authors, the stylistic variety of the original inevitably comes through. Conversely, if the guiding standard is a given level of modern English, uniformity of style quickly settles in.

A reviewer of the NEB voices exactly this objection. By replacing "Greek constructions and idioms by those of contemporary English," writes the reviewer, "they have largely 'ironed out' what is distinctive as between one part of the New Testament and another." Here is one example among others cited by this reviewer: "the differences in style between the Prologue to St Luke's Gospel, the same evangelist's account of the birth of John the Baptist, and a specimen narrative chapter from the end of Acts are . . . less striking in the new version" than in earlier translations.[3]

LOSS OF CONFIDENCE THAT ENGLISH READERS KNOW WHAT THE BIBLICAL AUTHORS WROTE

Advocates of dynamic equivalence belittle the validity of the longstanding distinction between what a biblical author says and what he means. The reviewers, however, correctly believe that the distinction is valid (just as Raymond Van Leeuwen does in a more recent review article in which he writes that "it is hard to know what the Bible *means* when we are uncertain about what it *says*").[4] A reviewer of the NEB thus asserts that "if one's sole concern is with what the New Testament writers mean, it is excellent. It is otherwise if one wants to find out what the documents actually say."[5]

The problem exists because dynamic equivalent translators give readers no clue that they have added to the original text. A reviewer thus protests that "there are many places where the new translation is a periphrasis or even a comment, rather than a translation."[6] Writes another reviewer, "It at once becomes clear that the new Bible departs . . . from the literal Greek."[7]

LOSS OF APPROPRIATE DIGNITY

A chorus of protest arose from reviewers of modernizing translations in regard to the informality and lack of dignity that the new translations embody. The most famous instance is T. S. Eliot's attack on the NEB. Eliot writes, "We ask in alarm: 'What is happening to the English language?' "[8] Eliot is not protesting the shrinking of the English vocabulary of the Bible but its tone, which Eliot labels a "combination of the vulgar, the trivial, and the pedantic."

Other reviewers agree. F. L. Lucas claims that "the danger with modernizers is that they can become crude, uncouth. . . . Too often it is as if they were officiating in Westminster Abbey in shirtsleeves; as if they were brightening Shakespeare's 'Canst thou not minister to a mind diseas'd?' into 'Aren't you a psychiatrist?' " In commenting on the reduction of the Bible to everyday colloquial speech, Lucas comments that this "kind of familiarity, too, can breed contempt."[9]

LOSS OF EFFECTIVENESS IN ORAL READING AND HEARING

It is no surprise that T. S. Eliot, a champion of what he called "the auditory imagination," would object to the loss of orality in modern translations that abandon the King James fluency. If the NEB were read only by solitary individuals, writes Eliot, it "would be merely a symptom of the decay of the English language in the middle of the 20th century. But the more it is adopted for religious services the more it will become an active agent of decadence." Eliot laments what happens when ministers ignore the way in which the "music of the phrase, of the paragraph, of the period is an essential constituent of good English prose," and also the degree to which the public reading of the liturgy depends on the "music of the spoken word."[10]

Other reviewers agree. One writes that the contemporary idiom used in the NEB "has lost the resonance of 'declaimed' speech, and is in many places thin and echo-less for reading aloud, especially in a church or during a service."[11] Dwight Macdonald likewise believes that an obvious defect in contemporizing translations is "the alteration of rhythm," an alteration that is debilitating to a book that is read aloud as often as the Bible is. "Quite aside from literary grace," writes Macdonald, "the ceremonial effect of the Bible is enhanced by the interesting, varied, and suitable rhythms of K.J.V."[12] For Dorothy Thompson, too, "the rhythms of the King James version are badly marred by modernizing the speech."[13]

LOSS OF VERBAL BEAUTY AND APHORISTIC MEMORABILITY

Partly because of its inherent style, and partly because of its longevity of use, the KJV was for centuries the gold standard for beauty of language. In general, modern translators who abandon the King James tradition do not want their translations to be beautiful.

It is no surprise, then, that T. S. Eliot laments that modern translations "lack the verbal beauty of the Authorised Version."[14] C. L. Wrenn observes that "so much of our natural speech is flat, trivial and unstable," and yet modern translations have opted for it.[15] Writes another reviewer, "Although Paul is clear [in the NEB] he loses his power of epigram."[16]

The King James Bible is the most aphoristic book of the English-speaking world, and the easiest from which to memorize. Virtually all of that is lost in modern translations that depart from the mainstream tradition. A colloquial Bible "does slip more smoothly into the modern ear," writes Dwight Macdonald, "but it also slides out more easily; the very strangeness and antique ceremony of the old forms make them linger in the mind."[17]

FAILURE OF TONE

The diminishment of language and verbal beauty of course affects the tone of the Bible. Reviewers protest this bitterly. Henry Gifford contrasts a series of passages from the NEB to the KJV and then concludes that "ultimately the tone is at fault."[18] For example, the KJV's "Be not deceived; God is not mocked" is replaced by "Make no mistake about this: God is not to be fooled." "What think ye of Christ?" has become "What is your opinion about the Messiah?"

The failure of tone is so glaring that multiple reviewers quote from a modern translation and then identify where we might expect

92

to find such a formulation in modern life (but emphatically not in the biblical world):

- "It sounds like a Chairman summing up after a long discussion."[19]
- It sounds like a "Ministry of Education circular, 'Notes towards the definition of postgraduate levels'."[20]
- "It sounds like my cat-loving maiden aunt shooing dogs away from the garden."[21]
- "It is the language of administrators, and even drops to that of politicians."[22]
- "It sounds like a schoolmaster's end-of-term report on a pupil's behaviour."[23]

Dwight Macdonald uses phrases such as "robbed of its earnest gravity" and "inappropriately brisk."[24] Stanley Edgar Hyman finds the tone of the NEB "often quite ludicrous."[25]

LOSS OF EXALTATION, AFFECTIVE POWER, AND A SENSE OF AUTHORITY

Such formal qualities as dignified language and sonorousness and smooth rhythm result in a sense of exaltation and affective power. When the language and rhythm are flat, those effects dissipate. Advocates of the King James style lament that loss. As a baseline we need to be aware that, in the words of John Livingston Lowes, "The language of elevated thought or feeling is always rhythmic. Strong feeling of whatever sort . . . imposed upon speech a rhythmic beat. . . . The Biblical literature, to an almost unrivalled degree, is profoundly tinged with feeling."[26] The reviewers lament the loss of affective power that accompanies strong rhythm.

One writes that "it is principally a loss of rhythm, and thus of the passions and sensibility that were expressed through that rhythm."[27] Another reviewer writes, "Almost everything has been lost: not only the rhythm, but the sense of authority that goes with it."[28]

Of course diminished vocabulary also contributes to the loss of authority in modernizing translations. "Modern English," writes Henry Seidel Canby in a discussion of informal Bible translations, "is lacking in eloquence, in its root sense of speaking out, and its acquired meaning of speaking out from the heart."[29]

LOSS OF MYSTERY AND THE NUMINOUS

Underlying all of the points just discussed is the question of what language is required to express and embody spiritual reality. C. L. Wrenn has stated the case best. Wrenn begins by noting that "in all languages I know of it has been the universal tendency to express the central ideas of religion in a language more dignified, more archaic even, and with more implicit levels of meaning than that used for the doings of ordinary life."[30] That being the case, modernizing Bible translations have produced "a spiritual contraction" in English-speaking society. The final conclusion: "If passages of the Scriptures are to suggest things of supra-phenomenal reality, it cannot well be done in the natural vocabulary of our current speech."[31]

Dwight Macdonald expresses the same opinion: religious language, writes Macdonald, is "connotative rather than direct, suggestive rather than explicit." To translate the Bible into the idiom of everyday conversation is "to flatten out, tone down, and convert into tepid expository prose what in K.J.V. is wild, full of awe, poetic, and passionate."[32] The everyday language of modernizing translations, claims Stanley Edgar Hyman, "is woefully inadequate for the ecstatic language of the mystery of John's Gospel." He adds that there are "many things that modern readers expect of a Bible besides clarity. One is majesty. . . . Another quality that can fairly be demanded of a Bible is mystery, much of which evaporates in the prosiness" of modernizing translations.[33]

SUMMARY

For Bible readers who have had no genuine experience of the historic mainstream of English Bible translation, the points raised by the reviewers may seem unimportant and perhaps even unintelligible. For those who have tasted of the King James tradition, the reviewers raise all the right objections to modernized translations.

PART THREE

The English Standard Version:
Heir to the Great Tradition

10

What the Preface to the English Standard Version Tells Us

The number of Bible readers who read and understand the prefaces to English Bible translations is statistically insignificant. I myself did not read such prefaces until I began writing books on English Bible translation. For the uninitiated, the technical matters discussed in these prefaces, along with the specialized vocabulary used in them, are a mystery.

However, for people who have been initiated into the issues involved in Bible translation, the prefaces to the various versions are a gold mine of information. For those who have "ears to hear," these prefaces are a road map to the translation that follows. In the complexity of the current scene, what is left *unsaid* can be as telling as what is said.

The preface to the English Standard Version (ESV) does not leave anything unsaid. It is a shorthand capsule that summarizes what I cover in the other parts of this book. The preface plants a series of "flags" that situate the ESV in the landscape of current English Bible translation. The purpose of this chapter is to unpack the specific assertions that the preface to the ESV makes. The material falls naturally into ten parts.

"THE CLASSIC MAINSTREAM OF ENGLISH BIBLE TRANSLATIONS"

I showed in an earlier chapter that dynamic equivalent translators are at pains to distance themselves from the King James Version (KJV) and by extension with a whole tradition that shares the qualities of the KJV. By contrast, the preface to the ESV sends numerous signals that its translators want to be associated with the mainstream tradition.

The opening paragraph begins with the engaging historical note that in English coronation ceremonies an English Bible is handed to the new monarch with a stately pronouncement. The point is then made that those very words echo a sentence in the introductory material of the King James Bible of 1611, which states that "God's sacred Word . . . is that inestimable treasure that excelleth all the riches of the earth."

That is only the beginning of the links drawn between the ESV and the tradition with which it is aligned. We read in the second paragraph that the ESV "stands in the classic mainstream of English Bible translations over the past half-millennium." The goal of the ESV is "to carry forward this legacy for a new century." Further, "The words and phrases themselves grow out of the Tyndale–King James legacy."

"THE LIVELY ORACLES OF GOD"

Underlying the ESV is a view of the Bible as God's Word. The preface quotes with approval the statement from the English corona-

100

tion ceremony that the Bible is "the lively Oracles of God." "This assessment of the Bible," the preface asserts, "is the motivating force behind the publication of the English Standard Version." Late in the preface we read that the hundred-member team that produced the ESV "shares a common commitment to the truth of God's Word and to historic orthodoxy."

As noted earlier in this book, viewing the Bible as God's inspired word leads some translation committees to believe that they are not free to change what the biblical authors wrote as part of the translation process, whereas other translators who embrace an evangelical view of Scripture do not feel the same curb on the translation process. The ESV belongs to the first of these two categories.

"To Avoid Overlooking Any Nuance of the Original Text"

Essentially literal translations possess an immediate advantage: because the translators are governed by the principle of reproducing the very words of the original text (as translated into English), these translations preserve the fullness of meaning in the original text. Translators who embrace an essentially literal philosophy do not reduce possible meanings to a single meaning by the way they translate a word or passage. They do not replace the multiplicity of meaning inherent in images and figures of speech with a propositional statement that has the effect of imposing a single interpretation on the image.

The preface to the New King James Version uses the phrase *full equivalence* to express the methodology of essentially literal translation. What this means is that everything that is in the original text is preserved in the English translation. Another formula by which to express this is that essentially literal translations preserve the *full exegetical potential* of the biblical text. While that phrase does not appear in the preface to the ESV, this is what is in view when we read that the Hebrew and Greek words of the original text were analyzed in a way that would "avoid under-translating or overlooking any nuance of the original text." In a later statement we read that the translators "have sought to capture the echoes and overtones of meaning that are so abundantly present in the original texts."

"FAITHFULNESS TO THE TEXT"

The hallmark of the ESV is that it is, as the preface states, an "essentially literal" text. The preface unpacks what this means. First, an essentially literal translation "seeks as far as possible to capture the precise wording of the original text." Further, "The emphasis is on 'word-for-word' correspondence." But the sentence does not stop there; it adds, "at the same time taking into account differences of grammar, syntax, and idiom between current literary English and the original languages." This qualification is important because one of the myths surrounding an essentially literal translation is that it is always *totally* literal.

A common formula by which to express the principle underlying essentially literal translation is "verbal equivalence," meaning that the translators have provided the equivalent English word or phrase for everything that is in the original text. The preface to the ESV uses an equally accurate formula—"formal equivalence." This means that the forms of the original, chiefly the words but also, where possible, the phraseology and word order of the original text are represented in the English translation. The ESV claims to be "as literal as possible while maintaining clarity of expression and literary excellence."

As an extension of this commitment to reproduce in English what the original text says, the ESV retains theological vocabulary as it has appeared in English Bibles since Tyndale. Some modern translations deliberately avoid theological vocabulary. By contrast, the ESV retains words such as *justification, sanctification, redemption, regeneration,* and *propitiation* "because of their central importance for Christian doctrine and also because the underlying Greek words were already becoming key words and technical terms in New Testament times."

CONCORDANCE: "THE SAME ENGLISH WORD FOR IMPORTANT RECURRING WORDS IN THE ORIGINAL"

The most obvious difference between the KJV and the ESV centers on the issue known today as concordance. Concordance in this case means using the same English word for a given Hebrew or Greek word every time (or nearly every time) it occurs in the Bible. Concordance was a high priority for the ESV translators. This was inevitable because of the commitment to verbal equivalence.

The King James translators did their work at a moment in history when the English language was expanding at an unprecedented rate and when excitement about the burgeoning possibilities of language ran high. It was a time of lexical and linguistic exhilaration. This is the context for the famous statement about synonyms that appears in the preface to the KJV: "We have not tied ourselves to a uniformity of phrasing, or to an identity of words. . . . ; as for example, if we translated the Hebrew or Greek word once by *Purpose*, never to call it *Intent*; if one where *Journeying*, never *Travelling.* . . . We cannot follow a better pattern for elocution than God himself; therefore he using divers words in his holy writ. . . . we . . . may use the same liberty in our English versions out of Hebrew and Greek." The decision to multiply synonyms reflects Renaissance exuberance over words and is not governed by fidelity to the biblical text. It is my impression that the decision of the King James translators to provide variety rather than consonance for a given Hebrew or English word makes the KJV a less literal translation than it otherwise would have been.

The ESV parts company with the KJV on this issue. The goal of the translators was to maintain as much concordance as possible (only occasionally departing from it). The preface states, "We have sought to use the same English word for important recurring words in the original."

There is a complex additional dimension to concordance, namely, making New Testament quotations from the Old Testament as parallel as the original text allows. The ESV translators strove for concordance on this matter also. In the words of the preface, "As far as grammar and syntax allow, we have rendered Old Testament passages cited in the New in ways that show their correspondence."

"THE STYLISTIC VARIETY OF THE BIBLICAL WRITERS"

The primary allegiance of an essentially literal translation is to the words of the original text. This is in contrast to many modern translations that highlight the concept of a "target audience" in their prefaces. The composite portrait of the target audience that emerges from the prefaces of modernizing translations is a person with the linguistic abilities of a sixth grader, with a taste only for the language of everyday conversational discourse, with little or no ability to interpret literature, and lacking facility or interest in theological matters. If a translation is governed by those presuppositions, the style of the Bible inevitably becomes a uniform style. But if an English translation sticks with what the original biblical authors wrote, the result is a many-splendored stylistic variety. The preface to the ESV accurately claims that variety is a feature of its translation: "The ESV lets the stylistic variety of the biblical writers fully express itself." That assertion is followed by a brief catalog of varied genres and styles in the Bible—flowing narrative, the figurative abundance of biblical poetry, the rhetorical flourishes of the prophets, the logic of Paul.

"Transparent to the Original Text"

The effect of the foregoing qualities of the ESV is that the text is "transparent to the original text." In fact, this is the goal of the ESV, and reaching that goal requires the methods delineated above.

To be transparent to the original text is simple. It requires translators to be faithful to the Hebrew and Greek texts of the original. What this means is that every attempt has been made to remove all obstacles that keep us from seeing what the biblical authors wrote. The translation practices of dynamic equivalence that create obstacles to seeing the original text fall into the following three categories, each accompanied by an illustration:

- Changing what the original text says as a way of updating it: whereas in the rural milieu of Bible times people tended to view everything nonrural as being a "city," dynamic equivalent translators often use the terms that we would use, namely, *town* or *village*, thereby obscuring the mind-set of the original author and audience.
- Substituting something in place of what is in the text, again usually as a way of making ancient details modern: replacing the command of Ecclesiastes 9:8 not to let "oil be lacking on your head" (ESV) with, for example, the substitute command to put on "a splash of cologne" (NLT).
- Omitting something from the biblical text because it is strange to modern experience or taste: dropping the metaphor from the statement of Psalm 1:1 that the godly person does not, as the ESV says, sit "in the seat of scoffers" (where the metaphor refers to serving on the policy-making body of a community).

I can imagine that doing these things might not immediately seem like putting an obstacle between the reader and what is in the original text, but upon analysis it is obvious that this is what is happening. Maneuvers like these divert a reader from the actual properties of the text and ancient world of the author and his audience, in effect short-circuiting the journey to the world of the original text.

The preface to the ESV states the formula of transparency to the original text in two different contexts. One is in connection with the style of the original biblical text: the ESV "seeks to be transparent to the original text, letting the reader see as directly as possible the structure and meaning of the original." The second context is a discussion of gender language: "In each case the objective has been transparency to the original text, allowing the reader to understand the original on its own terms rather than on the terms of our present-day culture."

"SIMPLICITY, BEAUTY, AND DIGNITY OF EXPRESSION"

The principles that I have explored thus far will seem compelling to someone who accepts the translation philosophy that under-girds them. Adherents of the rival translation philosophy will be unmoved. But when we turn our attention to the topic of literary excellence, translations in the mainstream tradition can prove their claims to superiority. I have yet to see a serious claim set forward for the literary excellence of dynamic equivalent and colloquial Bible translations.

That the ESV inherits the literary merits of the KJV (via the RSV, which was the starting point for the ESV) is so self-evident that the preface to the ESV can afford to understate the case. An early statement in the preface asserts that the criteria of faithfulness to the original text and accuracy in translating the text into English "were combined with simplicity, beauty and dignity of expression." For anyone familiar with what is currently said about the KJV, whether in praise or disparagement, it is immediately evident that these three descriptors are a reference to the King James tradition.

The preface proceeds to keep the subject of literary style in our awareness. We read that "the words and phrases themselves grow out of the Tyndale–King James legacy." Again: "Throughout, our goal has been to retain the depth of meaning and enduring language that have made their indelible mark on the English-speaking world." That, too, is an implied claim for continuity with the literary style of the KJV, as anyone familiar with current discussions of the KJV will recognize at once (especially in the phrase *enduring language*).

There are further submerged references to the style of the KJV. The dignified and smooth-flowing King James style automatically produces a beautiful-sounding Bible when it is read orally. The repeated adjective used for this quality, especially by debunkers who dislike the dignified language of the KJV, is *sonorous*. The preface to the ESV gestures toward this subject when it claims that "with its emphasis on literary excellence, the ESV is . . . suited for public reading and preaching."

The final effect of the stylistic superiority of the KJV is that it is the easiest of all English translations to memorize. By staying as close to the King James cadences and aphoristic brilliance as the updating of language and grammar allows, the ESV lives up to the claim of the preface that the ESV is ideally "suited . . . for Scripture memorization."

"IN THE AREA OF GENDER LANGUAGE"

On the issue of gender language, the ESV was at no point governed by the current debate on gender. Its retention of some (but not all) masculine references was determined solely by a commitment "to render literally what is in the original." Having stated that principle, the preface proceeds to spell out the technicalities of where the masculine was retained (for the generic reference to humans and in situations where the term refers to men rather than women) and where it was replaced by gender-neutral terminology (where the original text clearly refers to both men and women).

The nuances of gender language lie beyond my purpose here. What matters most is that the decisions reached by the ESV translation committee were based on its essentially literal philosophy of translation. Some modern translations are fueled by a feminist social agenda in their handling of gender language. The ESV is not motivated by any social agenda. The sole governing principle is "transparency to the original text."

"Textual Basis"

The preface becomes highly technical when discussing the text and manuscripts on which the translation is based. Two things to note are that (1) the Masoretic text has become the preferred Hebrew text for the Old Testament (a shift that occurred after the RSV), and (2) the ESV translators used the Greek texts and lexicons that reflect the current scholarly consensus. Also important are the scholarly footnotes that appear in the ESV. They fall mainly into two categories: (1) a recording of legitimate alternate readings for how a word is translated in the main text of the ESV and (2) an explanation of the difficulty of a given word in the original text or a technical term in the original text.

A hidden story lies behind the statement of the preface that the ESV team "benefited greatly from the massive textual resources that have become readily available recently." This statement perhaps means more to me as a literary scholar than it does to a biblical scholar with expertise in the Hebrew and Greek texts. When serving on the translation committee of the ESV, I was dazzled by the specialized knowledge that the biblical scholars on the committee possess. My discipline of literary criticism has nothing to compare with the quantity of technical knowledge that my biblical colleagues on the committee have in their minds and at the "tips of their fingers." This is greatly magnified by the resources available on the computer.

SUMMARY

As I spent more and more time with the preface to the ESV while composing this chapter, it emerged as a truly outstanding document. All that one needs to say about the ESV appears in kernel form in the preface. In turn, one paragraph immediately leaped out at me as encapsulating the preface. The paragraph is as follows:

> As an essentially literal translation, then, the ESV seeks to carry over every possible nuance of meaning in the original words of Scripture into our own language. As such, it is ideally suited for in-depth study of the Bible. Indeed, with its emphasis on literary excellence, the ESV is equally suited for public reading and preaching, for private reading and reflection, for both academic and devotional study, and for Scripture memorization.

11

THE CONTENT OF THE ENGLISH
STANDARD VERSION

The purpose of this book is to explain the nature of the English Standard Version (ESV) by showing its relation to the tradition to which it belongs. That tradition is what the preface to the ESV calls the "classic mainstream of English Bible translations." The greatness of the ESV is inseparable from the greatness of the tradition on which it draws. The first half of this book demonstrated the features of that tradition, and the chapter just before this one showed in detail the ways in which the ESV claims to align itself with that tradition. All that remains is to prove that the ESV lives up to its claims and to illustrate what that means.

My arrangement of material in the concluding four chapters is based on a distinction between form and content that has been at the heart of literature and its study since time immemorial. Content means the substance of the writing—*what* is said. Form refers to *how* that content is embodied and expressed.

The Root of the Matter: Verbal Equivalence

The content of the ESV—*what* the translation says—is dictated by the translation philosophy on which the translation rests. That philosophy goes by the following names:

- essentially literal translation
- fidelity to the words of the original
- verbal equivalence
- word-for-word translation

Although the word *equivalence* has been monopolized by the dynamic equivalence camp, I increasingly find myself gravitating toward its use for the philosophy that I embrace. I can think of four advantages to using the formula *verbal equivalence*.

First, it gets around an objection that can technically be raised against the word *literal*. From one point of view, no translation is literal, since it substitutes words from English in place of the Hebrew and Greek words of the original text. This does not negate an essential truth conveyed by the word *literal*, but unfortunately the word has been used by dynamic equivalent advocates to score an illusory point with a certain segment of the public, namely, that an essentially literal translation is an impossibility.

Second, while the concept of being *faithful to the words of the original* also expresses the truth of the matter, even translators who produce free translations and paraphrases claim to be true to the words of the original. In my view this is a false claim, but its effect is again to impair the usefulness of this formulation.

Third, there is also a liability to the formula expressed as "word-for-word." Strictly speaking, an essentially literal translation like the ESV does not always give us a single English word for every word in the original text. It sometimes gives multiple words or a phrase. On other occasions it uses a single English word for several words in the original. Additionally, the idea of "word-for-word" might be construed as transliteration, which is not what an essentially literal translation is.

Finally, the accuracy of the formula expressed as "verbal equivalence" commends it as a solution to the problems I have noted. An English translation always gives us an English *equivalent* for what the original Hebrew or Greek says. And it is a *verbal* equivalent in the sense that the translation has something in English for every word in the original.

The translation philosophy of verbal equivalence is rooted in a view of the Bible known as plenary inspiration (also called verbal inspiration). This view of Scripture asserts a belief that the words of the Bible, and not just its ideas, were inspired by God. Out of dozens of excellent formulations that exist, I have chosen this summary of the doctrine by J. I. Packer: "The point that *plenary* and *verbal* make is that the biblical words themselves (in Hebrew, Aramaic or Greek) are to be seen as God-given. . . . The Lord who gave the Word also gave the words . . . (2 Timothy 3:16; cf. 2 Peter 1:21). It is critically important, therefore, that . . . we make certain that we know what the God-given words are. Words, after all, are the vehicles and guardians of meaning; if we lose the words, we shall have lost the sense too."[1]

Some dynamic equivalent translators see no contradiction between the doctrine of verbal inspiration and their practices as translators, but I do see a contradiction. If the very words of Scripture are inspired, an English reader needs to see those words in the translation.

LIVING UP TO THE MAINSTREAM TRADITION

In earlier parts of this book, I delineated how the mainstream tradition accepted the premise of verbal equivalence. What does it mean that the ESV aligns itself with the King James tradition on this point? It means that with any passage that we read, we are being given an equivalent English word or phrase for everything in the original text. I am reminded of the comment of a preacher who uses the Revised Standard Version (the starting point for the ESV): that he enjoyed using that translation because he could "see the Greek behind the text." I cannot think of a higher commendation for a translation.

This explains, too, why the ESV enjoys a higher percentage of use on seminary campuses than in the broad cross section of the evangelical world. The original Hebrew and Greek texts are important to seminary students, who sense at once the superior accuracy of the ESV over dynamic equivalent translations. In an appendix to my book *Understanding English Bible Translation,* I quote testimonials from Bible teachers and expository preachers who put no confidence in dynamic equivalent translations because they are not accurate in the way that genuine Bible teaching and expository preaching require.

When Philip Ryken preached through the book of Galatians, he used the New International Version (NIV) because it was the Bible in the pew. When he polished his sermons for publication as a commentary, he was able to use the ESV. He found that he could eliminate virtually all of the instances where he had been forced to use the formula "now what the original actually says is . . ." in correction of the NIV.

To illustrate what a philosophy of verbal equivalence actually produces, I could simply quote at random from the text of the ESV. That would be a fruitless exercise. To give the matter significance, we need to set the ESV text alongside translations based on dynamic equivalence. Then we suddenly see what an essentially literal translation is.

There is another reason why I need to take a comparative approach. When a former Bible professor at Wheaton College polled his students in regard to Bible translations, he found that most of them began with the premise that all translations are equally accurate, and that all a reader needs to do is choose the one that he or she "likes best." We need to see that all translations are not equally accurate.

As an organizing framework, I will show how the translation philosophy of verbal equivalence enables the ESV to avoid three common practices of dynamic equivalent translators.

Accept No Substitutes

One of the standard ploys of dynamic equivalent translators is to substitute something in place of what is in the original. This was forced on my awareness when I was reading Gerald Hammond's book *The Making of the English Bible*. We have become so indoctrinated by the claims of dynamic equivalent advocates that we are lulled into acquiescence in regard to the word *equivalence*. I was jolted out of my stupor when Hammond suddenly asserted that dynamic equivalence "is not translation at all but merely replacement."[2] The freer the translation, the more open it is to this designation.

Out of curiosity, I turned to Song of Solomon 1:2. In verbal equivalence (not dynamic equivalence), it reads, "Let him kiss me with the kisses of his mouth!" (ESV). The King James Version (KJV) is identical, which is relevant to my claim throughout this book that the nature and excellence of the ESV come from its adherence to the mainstream tradition before it. The formula "with the kisses of his mouth" is not how we would say it (the omnipresent criterion of dynamic equivalent translators), but it is either a Hebrew idiom or a metaphor invented by the poet that does a good job of capturing the physical reality of a passionate kiss.

Translators who are not committed to translating what the poet actually wrote are uneasy with the unfamiliarity of the phrase "kisses of his mouth." So some of them give us substitutes. The New Living Translation (NLT) turns the wish or longing ("let him") into a direct command, and it throws the emphasis on a one-two repetition of kisses rather than the physical sensation evoked by "kisses of his mouth": "Kiss me and kiss me again." The Contemporary English Version pushes the line in an entirely different direction: "Kiss me tenderly!" The New English Bible throws the emphasis on a frenzy of kisses (not just the double kiss favored by the NLT), and it replaces the format of the wish ("let him . . .") by making the woman's song the motivation for the king's kisses: "I will sing the song of all songs to Solomon / *that he may smother me with kisses*" (italics added).

Gerald Hammond uses this verse in its various translations as his first example of how modernizing translations distort what the biblical authors actually wrote. "In rejecting the alien and introducing the familiar," writes Hammond, "it has ceased to be a translation." Again, "to translate meaning while ignoring the way that meaning has been articulated is not translation at all but merely replacement—murdering the original instead of recreating it."[3]

James 1:18 affords another illustration. The ESV renders it, "Of his own will he brought us forth by the word of truth, that we should be a kind of firstfruits of his creatures." The reference to firstfruits is a richly evocative allusion to the Old Testament ceremonial laws, turned to metaphoric use by James. (I will explore the multiple meanings of the metaphor below.)

If translators start with the twin premises that (1) the words of the original can be abandoned during the process of translating and (2) nothing in a translation should require readers to take time to figure something out or conduct research into what a statement means, then an allusion and metaphor such as firstfruits becomes a candidate for removal. That is what the following translations have done:

116

- "And we, out of all creation, became his prized possession" (NLT).
- ". . . showing us off as the crown of all his creatures" (MESSAGE).
- "He wanted us to be his own special people" (CEV).
- ". . . so we might be the most important of all the things he made" (NCV).
- ". . . that we should have first place among all his creatures" (GNB).

All of these translations have replaced the image of firstfruits with substitutes—prized possession, crown, special people, "most important," first place. They do not give us an equivalent but a replacement.

Gerald Hammond correctly notes that "now that the initial break has been made" from the original text by dynamic equivalence Bibles, we find each venture "moving us further away from the original text."[4] The result is that translation committees often hand us a substitute Bible, a stricture that an essentially literal translation like the ESV avoids. To adapt a familiar advertising slogan, a Bible reader should "accept no substitutes."

Sins of Omission

A second common license that dynamic equivalent translators take is to omit material from the original text. The rationale for doing so is that if something in the original is deemed difficult for a modern reader, removing the obstacle will make the Bible more immediately accessible. The largest category of such omission occurs with the poetry and poetic language of the Bible, including metaphors and figures of speech found in prose passages such as the epistles.

Psalm 87:7 can serve as an illustration of how this happens. The ESV renders the last phrase this way: "All my springs are in you" (KJV *thee*, but otherwise identical), with the *you* referring to the city of Jerusalem (called Zion in the poem). We can compare that to the following three renditions:

- "I too am from Zion" (CEV).
- "All good things come from Jerusalem" (NCV).
- "In Zion is the source of all our blessings" (GNB).

Obviously the metaphor of *springs* has been removed from sight, and English-speaking readers have no way of knowing that the omission has occurred unless they consult an essentially literal translation.

A famous archetype in the New Testament is *walking* as a metaphor for the lifestyle and obedience to Christ that are engendered by the new birth. This metaphor is rooted in Old Testament poetry and wisdom literature, where the image of the path or way refers to the ongoing experience of life, to a person's general conduct, and to the consequences of conduct. This strikes me as an easy metaphor to grasp, with the added advantage of multiple meanings. Essentially literal translations of course retain the image: consider Romans 6:4 in the ESV: ". . . we too might walk in newness of life" (KJV similar).

But dynamic equivalent translators apparently think that the metaphor of *walking* is an impossible burden for modern readers, so many of them remove the image from the picture:

- ". . . we too may live a new life" (NIV).
- ". . . we also may live new lives" (NLT).
- ". . . so that we would live a new life" (CEV).

Several things need to be said here. First, who is the ultimate author of the image of *walk* in the New Testament passages where it appears? If one accepts an evangelical view of scriptural inspiration, the answer is that the Holy Spirit is the author. Raymond Van Leeuwen writes in this regard that "the translator who removes biblical metaphors to make the text 'easier' for readers may defeat the purpose of the Holy Spirit, who chose a metaphor in the first place."[5] Second, the New Testament authors *had the lexical resources* to say *live* instead of *walk*. They chose the latter. To drop their metaphor is to violate what they intended.

Third, an example like this highlights the sense of superiority that dynamic equivalent translators assume vis-à-vis the biblical authors. The unstated premise is that the translators can say it better than the biblical authors said it. The writers of the epistles gave us the metaphor of *walk*, but the translators can "get it right" by dropping the metaphor.

Translation or Commentary?

A third common practice of dynamic equivalent translators is to add commentary beyond what the biblical authors wrote. Because of this practice, it is misleading to use the word *translation* for such Bibles. They are actually a translation plus a commentary plus the product of a heavy editorial hand in regard to style. Of course, the general reader has no way of knowing where translation stops and the other activities start.

Examples of this blurring of the line between translation and commentary occur on every page of dynamic equivalent Bibles. A literal rendition of Psalm 34:5 is that "those who look to him are radiant" (ESV). Here is how two dynamic equivalent translations add to what the psalmist wrote (italics show what is in effect added commentary):

- "*The oppressed* look to him and are *glad*" (GNB).
- "Those who look to him *for help* will be radiant *with joy*" (NLT).

Because essentially literal translators believe in fidelity to the words of the original, they pass on to English readers whatever demands and difficulties and even mysteries that the original authors put before *their* readers. "Have salt in yourselves" (Mark 9:50, KJV, ESV), Jesus commanded his listeners metaphorically and enigmatically. Dynamic equivalent translators are bent on moving from translation to commentary, as in the following examples (italics added to show the commentary that has been added to the original text):

- "Have the salt *of friendship among* yourselves" (GNB).
- "You *must* have *the qualities of* salt *among* yourselves" (NLT).
- "*Be preservatives* yourselves" (MESSAGE).

There is an incessant nervousness about the original here, a felt need to tamper with what the biblical authors wrote and to fix what is perceived as a problematical text.

Ideas have consequences. If a translation is based on the premise of verbal equivalence, certain features immediately become part of the actual translation. The ideas underlying dynamic equivalence produce something very different. It is important to note four further features of the content of the ESV and the tradition to which it belongs.

Full Exegetical Potential

First, the practice of adding commentary to the biblical text in the process of translation is almost always an exercise in reductionism. Multiple possible and/or legitimate meanings of a passage are reduced to the one preferred by a translation committee. Correspondingly, the range of meanings that a reader, a Bible teacher, or a preacher can legitimately find in the text shrinks in the process. The exegetical potential of the original text is complete in a literal translation and stripped down when a translator becomes a commentator or exegete.

We can see this in the metaphor of believers as firstfruits (James 1:18). Under Old Testament ceremonial laws, farmers brought a sacrifice in the form of the first produce or grain that a harvest produced. It was at once a gesture of thanksgiving to the God of provision and of faith that even though a farmer gave up ownership of the firstfruits there would still be enough for the family. Additionally, firstfruits represented something set apart in a special way for God. There was also the idea of anticipation: the firstfruits were first, and more was to follow. Here is a metaphor whose meanings keep expanding. But that fullness of exegetical potential evaporates when one-dimensional, reductionistic translations dole out just one meaning—or a substitute meaning: "prized possession"; "crown"; "special people"; "most important"; "first place."

Keeping the Biblical Text Stable

One of the advantages inherent in verbal equivalence is that translators have a built-in curb on how they translate the Bible. If translators do not feel free to depart from what the biblical authors wrote, they are at once prevented from wandering into speculative and reductionistic pathways. As a result, if we compare how translations in the Tyndale–King James tradition render a common passage, we find a remarkable degree of uniformity. Whatever variance exists is a lexical variance in keeping with what we might expect when translators wrestle with what English words best capture the words of the original text. I hinted at this when I noted the congruence of the ESV with the KJV in passages quoted earlier in this chapter.

By contrast, the variance found among dynamic equivalent translations produces the phenomenon of the destabilized text. By this I mean that readers of those translations find a bewildering array of contradictory readings of the same passage. In turn, this removes the incentive to ascertain what is actually the Word of God, since the experts do not even agree among themselves. Here is an example of a destabilized English Bible text—John 6:27:

- "For on him God the Father has placed his seal of approval" (NIV).
- ". . . for on him God the Father has set the seal of his authority" (REB).
- ". . . because God the Father has given him the right to do so" [no seal in view] (CEV).
- ". . . because on him God the Father has put his power" [again, no seal in view] (NCV).

While claiming to clarify the biblical texts, dynamic equivalent translations actually confuse readers when they start comparing dynamic equivalent translations with each other.

Respect for Biblical Authors

Essentially literal translations in the mainstream tradition do not look down on biblical authors as inept and pitiable people whose writing needs to be corrected. They do not wring their hands when biblical writers use metaphors and other figurative language. Essentially literal translators pay biblical authors the respect of assuming that they knew what they meant and wrote in keeping with their intention. I am going to hazard the guess that the omnipresent modern formula "what the biblical author was *trying to say*" did not exist before the rise of dynamic equivalent translations.

Inherent in the dynamic equivalent enterprise is the image of the biblical author as needing help. The preface to the NIV claims that the phrases *Lord of hosts* and *God of hosts* "have little meaning" for "most readers today." In other words, the biblical poets have let modern readers down. If the original text needs to be changed as continuously as dynamic equivalent translations change it, readers quickly get the impression that the biblical authors were an incompetent lot.

Respect for Bible Readers

The same thing carries over to how the rival translation philosophies picture Bible readers. The composite picture that emerges from the prefaces and surrounding documents of dynamic equivalent translations is a reader with sixth-grade lexical and syntactical abilities, a reader who struggles with poetry, a reader who cannot grasp theological language and concepts, and a reader who cannot be expected to rise above his or her present limitations in the areas I have just named.

The unstated premise of essentially literal translations in the King James tradition is that readers should be expected to rise to the level that the original Bible puts before them. If Paul or Jesus uses a metaphor, it is a fair inference that God wants readers to grapple with that metaphor. When they do, they see meanings that are not even available to them when a translation removes the metaphor from sight.

SUMMARY

This chapter has explored the content of the ESV. That content is based on the premise of verbal equivalence, which the ESV translators perpetuated from the King James tradition. The result is that English readers can have confidence that they are reading an English equivalent of the original text, not a substitute for it, and not a commentary on it.

12

THE LANGUAGE AND STYLE OF THE ENGLISH STANDARD VERSION

My own shorthand way of asserting the literary and stylistic excellence of the English Standard Version (ESV) is to say that the ESV rides the literary coattails of the King James Version (KJV). While the political metaphor of coattails may have negative connotations in some contexts, the formula of riding the literary coattails of the KJV is for me a supreme compliment to the ESV.

That formula fits my design for this book perfectly. I explored the stylistic qualities of the King James tradition at length in the first half of this book. Having done so, I feel no need to belabor the traits that I am about to illustrate as belonging to the ESV. The groundwork has been laid earlier in this book.

PRELIMINARIES

My journey through the literary and stylistic qualities of the ESV will be simplified if I plant four signposts at the outset of the journey. They are as follows:

First, *the ESV is not just like the KJV.* To say that the ESV rides the literary coattails of the KJV is not to claim that the ESV represents minimal departure from the King James Bible. The King James Bible is a Renaissance document. The ESV is a modern document. In fact, the starting point for the ESV was not the KJV but the Revised Standard Version (RSV). By my taste, one of the superiorities of the ESV over the New King James Version is that the latter is too tied to the KJV, with the result that it does not read like a twenty-first-century book.

Second, *the ESV perpetuates the principles but not the actual language of the KJV.* I found a comment by Alister McGrath particularly insightful on this matter. "There is no doubt that the King James Bible is a model English text," writes McGrath, but all translations "eventually require revision, not necessarily because they are defective, but because the language . . . itself changes over time." To remain overly tied to the KJV is to "betray the intentions and goals of those who conceived and translated it—namely, to translate the Bible into living English." On the logic of this, "the true heirs of the King James translators are those who continue their task today."[1]

This is exactly what the translators of the ESV have done. The ESV belongs to the Tyndale–King James *tradition*. It is not a "retouched" King James Bible. Instead it embodies *the principles* on which the KJV and its predecessors were based, but in modern English language and grammar.

Third, *it is primarily the stylistic flair of the KJV that flows into the ESV.* What carries over from the King James tradition is not so much the *language*, which has changed drastically, but certain *qualities*. These qualities do, indeed, make the ESV often sound like the KJV, a fact to be celebrated. The editor of an anthology of poems based on New Testament passages chose the RSV (starting point for the ESV) for the biblical passages, because the RSV "preserves almost all the phrases [i.e., phraseology] and cadences of the King James Version."[2]

Fourth, *the great divide: should an English Bible sound like everyday conversation?* At the level of *content*, the great debate is whether an English translation should reproduce the actual words of the original. The battle line changes when we turn to *style*. Here the question is whether a translation should be colloquial, and in particular whether it should match *spoken* language as we find it in informal settings today. There is no agreed-upon term by which to call the alternative to colloquialism, so I will use the term that is used in my own profession of English professors. What most college composition teachers teach in their courses is called standard formal English. The ESV is couched in standard formal English.

LANGUAGE

It does not trivialize English Bible translation to say that the most important ingredient in a Bible translation is its words. When we open a Bible, we find words on a page. At rock bottom, the reason one translation is better than another is that its language is better, starting with fidelity of that language to the words that the biblical authors used.

In contrast to my emphasis on words and language, advocates of dynamic equivalent Bibles demote form and language in deference to what they call meaning. Gordon Fee and Mark Strauss, for example, write that "accuracy concerns the *meaning* of the text rather than its form."[3] This is an obvious fallacy, because form *is* meaning. Without the form, the meaning does not exist. If we change the words, we change the meaning.

I have said the foregoing to establish the importance of the topic I am about to discuss, namely, the language of the ESV. That language is standard formal English—written English on its best behavior, pitched above colloquial conversation and above some (but not all) of what we find in the newspaper. To cite a parallel, the level of vocabulary and syntax used by television newscasters is pitched at a higher level than that of many of the people who are interviewed by these newscasters.

Prose Narrative

Straightforward narrative is well represented in the ESV by an account of Jesus's stilling of the sea (Mark 4:35–39):

> On that day, when evening had come, he said to them, "Let us go across to the other side." And leaving the crowd, they took him with them in the boat, just as he was. And other boats were with him. And a great windstorm arose, and the waves were breaking into the boat, so that the boat was already filling. But he was in the stern, asleep on the cushion. And they woke him and said to him, "Teacher, do you not care that we are perishing?" And he awoke and rebuked the wind and said to the sea, "Peace! Be still!" And the wind ceased, and there was a great calm.

The primary determinant of what we find here is what Mark himself wrote. No attempt is made to change it. Additionally, the translators did not slant the syntax toward the presumed reading ability of a sixth grader. Subordination of clauses appears instead of a series of short, choppy sentences.

The general tenor of language used in the ESV stands out more clearly if compared to other translations. In the ESV account, the disciples ask Jesus if he does not care that they "are perishing," whereas more colloquial versions render it as "about to die" (GNB); "if we drown" (NIV); and "going to drown" (NLT). In the ESV rendition, Jesus rebukes the waves with the awe-inspiring commands, "Peace! Be still!" Other translations give us: "Quiet! Be still!" (NIV); "Silence! Be still!" (NLT); "Jesus got up and ordered the wind and the waves to be quiet" (CEV).

Poetry

Poetry advertises its difference from ordinary prose discourse. It always possesses "arresting strangeness." This puts it on a collision course with translations that want to (1) reduce the language to a low linguistic level (sixth grade, for example) and (2) make everything sound "natural" (by which is meant oral and colloquial speech patterns). The ESV takes the high road and expects readers to rise to the level of the biblical poets themselves. Here are the first two verses of Psalm 24 in the ESV:

> The earth is the Lord's and the fullness thereof,
>> the world and those who dwell therein,
> for he has founded it upon the seas
>> and established it upon the rivers.

No one would mistake this for the language used at the local Walmart. By contrast, if translators begin with the premise that everything should sound "natural" (as Edwin Palmer of the NIV claimed to me in personal correspondence), they of course try to make the poetry of the original sound prose-like, as in the CEV rendition:

> The earth and everything on it
>> belong to the Lord.
> The world and its people
>> belong to him.
> The Lord placed it all
>> on the oceans and rivers.

Other leading modern translations pitch their poetry between the two poles I have illustrated above. The ESV, following in the train of the King James tradition, can be trusted to give us poetic language unencumbered with qualms that it does not sound like everyday conversational prose.

Oratory

The Bible is filled with formal addresses and prayers uttered on public occasions or in public places. The ESV belongs to the line of thinking that "high thoughts must have high language" (Greek dramatist Aristophanes). Here is the beginning of Solomon's prayer at the dedication of the temple (1 Kings 8:23–24): "O LORD, God of Israel, there is no God like you, in heaven above or on earth beneath, keeping covenant and showing steadfast love to your servants who walk before you with all their heart, who have kept with your servant David my father what you declared to him. You spoke with your mouth, and with your hand have fulfilled it this day." The ESV language is exalted because that was how the king of the nation actually spoke on the most solemn occasion of his life.

COMBINED SIMPLICITY AND MAJESTY

Unencumbered by the measuring stick of a target audience, the ESV is free to be as simple or majestic as the original biblical text is. The Bible is filled with passages that are simplicity personified: "In the beginning, God created the heavens and the earth. . . . And God said, 'Let there be light,' and there was light" (Gen. 1:1, 3, ESV). Of course with the Bible, the effect of such simplicity is majestic at the same time.

The style of historical narrative in the Bible tends toward simplicity in actual form and majesty of effect. Here is a specimen from the Gospels: "And immediately he left the synagogue and entered the house of Simon and Andrew, with James and John. Now Simon's mother-in-law lay ill with a fever, and immediately they told him about her. And he came and took her by the hand

and lifted her up, and the fever left her, and she began to serve them" (Mark 1:29–31).

At the other end of the stylistic continuum, we find numerous passages in the Bible that are "the highest of the high." The ESV does not scale back the high style of such passages. Most modern translations manage to damage the embellished style of Paul's encomium to love in 1 Corinthians 13, but the ESV carries right on from where the KJV left off: "If I speak in the tongues of men and of angels, but have not love, I am a noisy gong or a clanging cymbal. And if I have prophetic powers, and understand all mysteries and all knowledge, and if I have all faith, so as to remove mountains, but have not love, I am nothing" (vv. 1–2). Paul did not have a sixth-grade level of rhetoric or spiritual insight, so naturally he did not write like a sixth grader.

As I said in an earlier chapter, even though the KJV has passages at the two ends of the stylistic continuum, usually as we read we are faced with a blend of the simple and the majestic. The same is true of the ESV, as in this passage (Isa. 5:20):

> Woe to those who call evil good
> and good evil,
> who put darkness for light
> and light for darkness,
> who put bitter for sweet
> and sweet for bitter!

The words are all simple. The syntax and rhetorical patterning are complex and sophisticated, with the formal "woe" format, the strict parallelism of clauses, and the carefully orchestrated inversions arranged as chiasms (in which the same key words appear in pairs of lines, but in inverted order in the second line). All of these ingredients raise the effect far above the conversational idiom of the breakfast table.

APHORISTIC QUALITY

The King James Bible is the most aphoristic book that most English-speaking people know. It contains so many famous quotations that it sustains a book all by itself when its entries from *Bartlett's Familiar Quotations* are segregated out from that book.[4]

It is emphatically not true that modern translations just naturally preserve the memorable quality of the Bible's proverbs. One of my assignments when I teach Homer's *Odyssey* is to ask students to read around in the biblical book of Proverbs and find at least one apt proverb that sums up a major theme or viewpoint embodied in Homer's epic, with a view toward reading the proverb aloud in class. This assignment worked beautifully until the NIV hit the classroom. The first time this happened, I stood in the classroom in a state of shock as students read their supposed aphorisms. Many of them were not aphoristic at all but flat, insipid, prosaic statements. And that was before the onslaught of colloquial translations.

The ESV does not disappoint us in regard to preserving the aphoristic brilliance of the King James Bible. This was not an "official" policy of the ESV translation committee. It happened naturally because of the shared translation philosophy of these translators. If we ask what makes a statement aphoristic, the answer is that it does a variety of things with language that ordinary discourse does not, including tightness of syntax (the well–turned-phrase principle) and figurative language. Displacement of ordinary word order can also contribute.

I decided simply to collect some well-known aphorisms from the ESV and then check to see how closely they correspond to the KJV rendition. Here are the proverbs:

- "The fear of the LORD is the beginning of knowledge" (Prov. 1:7).
- "The name of the LORD is a strong tower; // the righteous man runs into it and is safe" (Prov. 18:10).

- "He who loves money will not be satisfied with money" (Eccles. 5:10).
- "Draw near to God, and he will draw near to you" (James 4:8).
- "Consider the lilies of the field, how they grow" (Matt. 6:28).

The only deviations from the KJV are these: the KJV has "the righteous runneth into it" in Proverbs 18:10; it has "silver" instead of "money" in the Ecclesiastes passage; and it has "nigh" instead of "near" in the passage from James. This confirms my thesis in this book: the greatness of the ESV is rooted in the greatness of the tradition to which it belongs, but even though it inherits a birthright of excellence from the KJV, it is not a makeover KJV.

EXALTATION AND AFFECTIVE POWER

The chapter in which I surveyed statements by reviewers about modernizing translations revealed the depth of revulsion that these reviewers felt toward the scaling down of the sense of exaltation that breathes from the pages of the KJV. The ESV does not step down the voltage so no fuses will blow (to use the metaphor of one of the reviewers). We can divide the material into various categories of passages.

In a class by themselves are passages that aspire toward the grand style. It takes a deliberate effort at colloquializing to destroy the effect, and the ESV does not take that turn. Here is an example of elevated language and syntax from Paul's address to the Areopagus in Athens, perhaps the most intellectually formal occasion on which Paul spoke: "Men of Athens, I perceive that in every way you are very religious. For as I passed along and observed the objects of your worship, I found also an altar with this inscription, 'To the unknown god.' What therefore you worship as unknown, this I proclaim to you. The God who made the world and everything in it, being Lord of heaven and earth, does not live in temples made by man" (Acts 17:22–24). This is not the place to analyze how Paul's address fits all of the formal rules of a Greek oration, but that is the case, and the ESV rendition answers to the exalted occasion and genre.

The "thanksgiving" sections of the New Testament epistles are among the most moving parts in the whole Bible. The ESV does not reduce the language and chop up the syntax into short sentences but instead lets the exaltation roll: "May you be strengthened with all power, according to his glorious might, for all endurance and patience with joy, giving thanks to the Father, who has qualified you to share in the inheritance of the saints in light" (Col. 1:11–12).

But affective power does not require an exalted vocabulary and features of the high style like the epithets in Paul's address to the Aeropagus or the flowing syntax of the epistolary thanksgiving. Jesus's Sermon on the Mount is an example of how simple vocabulary and sentence elements embellished by a heavy overlay of rhetorical patterns of repetition can elevate us: "Ask, and it will be given to you; seek, and you will find; knock, and it will be opened to you. For everyone who asks receives, and the one who seeks finds, and to the one who knocks it will be opened" (Matt. 7:7–8).

Of course when we praise the KJV and its heirs for their exaltation and power to elevate and move us, we primarily have the poetic parts of the Bible in mind. As exemplified in the following lines, the ESV retains the poetic power for which the KJV set the gold standard:

Bless the LORD, O my soul,
    and all that is within me,
    bless his holy name!
Bless the LORD, O my soul,
    and forget not all his benefits. . . .
Bless the LORD, O you his angels,
    you mighty ones who do his word,
    obeying the voice of his word!
Bless the LORD, all his hosts,
    his ministers, who do his will! (Ps. 103:1–2, 20–21)

Our imaginations and feelings and soul soar when we read such lines.

Style is substance. When we scale down the language of the Bible, we diminish its content. In my book *Understanding English Bible Translation,* I trace levels of reductionism that are evident with some test cases of what in the King James tradition is exalted.[5] Here is a summary (anyone wishing to know what translations are quoted should consult my book).

In the RSV Ruth is said by Boaz to be "a woman of worth" (Ruth 3:11), and in the ESV "a worthy woman." The NIV rendering "woman of noble character" maintains the elevated status of Ruth and the esteem in which Boaz holds her. As we move down the scale of increasing informality, the stature of Ruth shrinks in our imagination: "respected by everyone in town"; "a fine woman"; "a capable woman"; "a real prize."

My heart leaps when I read the comment that King Saul, when he was still on the ascendancy, surrounded himself with "men of valor whose hearts God had touched" (1 Sam. 10:26, RSV, ESV). My imagination deflates, and my exhilaration for these men dissipates, as I move down the continuum of modernizing translations: "powerful men"; "warriors"; "true and brave men"; "strong men"; "young men"; "fighting men"; "band of men."

If we want exaltation and affective power, we of course need to retain the *O, behold,* and *verily* constructions of the KJV and its predecessors. The ESV retains them, and our spirits soar: "Behold, I stand at the door and knock" (Rev. 3:20). That is awe-inspiring and emphatically not like what we hear in ordinary conversation. I will simply list what happens to the passage in other modern translations and refrain from expressing how I feel about them: "Here I am!" "Listen!" "Look!" "Look at me." By contrast: "Behold, I stand at the door and knock."

SUMMARY

In this chapter I have explored the same topics that I took up in the parallel chapter earlier in this book on the language and style of the Tyndale–King James tradition. All that I have needed to do in this chapter is take my examples from the ESV instead of the KJV. The principles remain intact. In the ESV the level of vocabulary matches that of a given passage in the original text. The ESV never scales down the vocabulary to match a target audience with assumed low reading abilities. It approximates the combined simplicity and majesty of the original Bible and KJV, and it is consistently aphoristic and therefore easy to memorize, as the KJV and RSV are as well. The ESV also exudes the exaltation and affective power of the KJV. The supreme compliment that I can pay the ESV is to say that it rides the literary coattails of the KJV.

13

RHYTHM AND FLUENCY IN THE
ENGLISH STANDARD VERSION

The oral effects of the King James Version (KJV) are matchless and cannot be duplicated. However, the rhythm and cadences of the KJV can be approximated in a modern translation if the translators follow the model of the KJV. The most provable superiority of the Revised Standard Version (RSV) and English Standard Version (ESV) over the New International Version (NIV) and its successors lies right here in the area of fluency. Smooth flow was not a priority of the NIV translators and modernizing versions after it. It *was* a priority in the ESV.

PRELIMINARIES

While the focus of this chapter will be on oral effects of the ESV, I want to assert that fluency registers in silent reading as well as oral reading. Prose and poetry that flow beautifully, as they do in the ESV, are easier and more pleasant to read even silently than are translations where the language bumps along in staccato fashion.

Additionally, it is wrong to think that rhythm is of concern only to specialists who can understand the technicalities of meter and phraseology. It is true that the explanation of exactly what produces good and bad rhythm is the domain of literary experts. But laypeople recognize bad rhythm intuitively. When I gave the NIV a negative review upon its appearance, the point with which the rank-and-file person resonated was my assertion of the lack of fluency. We do not need technical analysis to ascertain good and bad rhythm.

It would be wrong to think that a deficient flow of words and phrases is of negligible importance in an English Bible. On the contrary, rhythm is one of the most important criteria for a book that is read aloud. Good rhythm in a Bible translation is like a qualifying exam: if a translation does not measure up in this area, it is not in the running to be a superior Bible for public use. The ESV emphatically "measures up" in regard to rhythm and oral effects.

FLUENCY OF PROSE

The flow of prose is less structured than the metrical and line-by-line format of poetry. The sentence (not the line, as in poetry) is the recurrent unit of prose. In poetry the arrangement of accented and unaccented syllables dominates the flow, whereas in prose phraseology dominates. The thing that matters most in prose rhythm is the smooth, wavelike recurrence of words and phrases. When prose flows smoothly, our ear can catch the methodical rise and fall in the movement of the language. Much of this registers with us even in silent reading.

I will start with an example of simple narrative prose, which is the least complex of all genres in the Bible. Much to its credit, the ESV retains the conjunction *and* for the Hebrew *waw* and the Greek *kai*. Retaining this conjunction works wonders with the cadence of sentences. Here is a randomly selected specimen:

And Leah conceived and bore a son, and she called his name Reuben, for she said, "Because the LORD has looked upon my affliction; for now my husband will love me." She conceived again and bore a son, and said, "Because the LORD has heard that I am hated, he has given me this son also." And she called his name Simeon. Again she conceived and bore a son, and said, "Now this time my husband will be attached to me, because I have borne him three sons." Therefore his name was called Levi. (Gen. 29:32–34)

The statements march in businesslike progression, but the effect is fluid rather than abrupt and disjointed.

Here is how the passage appears when translators opt for short sentences and colloquial language (GNB):

Leah became pregnant and gave birth to a son. She said, "The LORD has seen my trouble, and now my husband will love me"; so she named him Reuben. She became pregnant again and gave birth to another son. She said, "The LORD has given me this son also, because he heard that I was not loved"; so she named him Simeon. Once again she became pregnant and gave birth to another son. She said, "Now my husband will be bound more tightly to me, because I have borne him three sons"; so she named him Levi.

The passage is not a rhythmic disaster; it simply lacks the fluency of the ESV.

The contrast becomes sharper when we move to a specimen of oratory. Here is a passage from Paul's encomium to love as it appears in the ESV: "Love is patient and kind; love does not envy or boast; it is not arrogant or rude. . . . Love bears all things, believes all things, hopes all things, endures all things" (1 Cor. 13:4–5, 7). The passage moves in a smooth flow of rising and falling cadence. The passage instills confidence and exuberance in a person who reads it orally. A listener likewise feels carried along on a beautiful stream.

The same is not true with translations that reduce the passage to a series of short, staccato statements:

- "Love is patient, love is kind. It does not envy, it does not boast, it is not proud. It does not dishonor others. . . . It always protects, always trusts, always hopes, always perseveres" (NIV).
- "Love is kind and patient, / never jealous, boastful, / proud, or rude. . . . / Love is always supportive, / loyal, hopeful, / and trusting" (CEV).

In these two passages the rhythmic beauty of the passage evaporates as we bump along.

POETIC RHYTHM

Rhythm and cadence are even more important when we move to poetry. Poetry aspires toward the quality of music unless it is deliberately or carelessly reduced to newspaper-like prose. To illustrate the point, I have chosen to repeat the same passages that I adduced in earlier chapters as examples of excellence in King James rhythm. These passages show that the ESV approximates the rhythmic effects of the KJV.

The rendition of Psalm 73:2 in the ESV is nearly identical with the rhythm of the KJV: "But AS for ME, my FEET had ALmost STUMBled, // my STEPS had NEARly SLIPPED." This is a model of iambic meter consisting of an unaccented syllable followed by an accented syllable. The New English Bible's rendition of the second line shows how smooth meter usually vanishes when translators opt for a colloquial style: "my foothold had all but given way." Or the NIV: "I had nearly lost my foothold."

In my chapter 5 excursion into the KJV, I noted that verses 3 and 6 of Psalm 23 fall into a predominantly anapestic meter. The ESV is likewise predominantly anapestic and smooth-flowing: "He [unaccented] reSTORES my SOUL. . . . And I [both unaccented] shall DWELL in the HOUSE of the LORD forEVer." The ESV translators had two great advantages when translating verses like these: (1) they began with the KJV and RSV as a baseline that was assumed to carry over unless there was a compelling reason to change it, and (2) they were opposed to a colloquial rendition and were spared the rhythmic infelicities that almost always accompany such colloquialism.

The archaic *eth* and *est* verb endings were an asset to the King James translators because such unaccented syllables help to produce a regular meter. The ESV lacks that resource, but it nonetheless proves that an English translation can perpetuate the smooth meter of the KJV even without the uninflected verb endings. Psalm 1:3 is an example: "In ALL that he DOES, he PROSpers." That rendition probably seems inevitable until we look at prose-like renditions:

- "They sucCEED in EVerything they DO" (GNB).
- "WhatEVer they DO [complete break] PROSpers" (NIV).
- "THOSE PEOple sucCEED in EVerything they DO" (CEV).

It is obvious that smooth rhythm is on the radar screen of some translation committees and not of others. It was on the radar screen of the ESV committee, where a verdict that "it sounds clunky to me" was often sufficient to steer the committee away from a contemplated rendition.

I will be content with one more example. The rhythm of the ESV in Psalm 24:1 is exemplary: "The EARTH is the LORD'S and the FULLness thereOF, / the WORLD and THOSE who DWELL thereIN." The rhythm of the following translations illustrates a quality that the King James translators (in their preface) called "halting":

- "The EARTH is the LORD'S, and EVerything IN IT, / the WORLD, and ALL who LIVE IN IT" (NIV).
- "The EARTH is the LORD'S, and ALL IT conTAINS, / The WORLD, and THOSE who DWELL IN IT" (NASB).
- "To the LORD beLONG the EARTH and EVerything IN IT, / The WORLD and ALL ITS inHABitants" (REB).

WHY FLUENCY MATTERS

It would be wrong to think that rhythm and smooth flow of words and phrases are minor issues. There are three reasons why fluency is important in an English Bible—and therefore why the ESV is a superior translation.

Good rhythm and smooth flow are essential to any text that is read orally. The Bible is preeminently an oral book, read aloud in public worship, on ceremonial occasions, and around the table. Whenever I hear a modernizing translation read orally, I experience a diminishment of effect and authority. To speak the truth, it angers me to see a birthright of excellence (the King James tradition) sold for something that is rhythmically inept. Beauty matters to God, and it should matter to Bible translators and Bible readers.

The smooth flow of words and phrases is an aid to memory as well as to oral reading. A line that flows smoothly is easier to memorize than a line that bumps along and impedes the flow of thought. Additionally, good rhythm often produces an aphoristic effect that (1) commands immediate attention and (2) sticks in the mind afterward. Literary critic F. L. Lucas, in lamenting what modern translations have done with the King James rendition, "Come unto me, all ye that labour and are heavy laden, and I will give you rest," comments that modernization "ruins the beauty of rhythm which has helped the memories of generations, and kept the Bible running in their heads."[1]

Finally, impassioned and heightened speech falls naturally into a rhythmic pattern. The loss of rhythmic fluency in modernizing translations is a symptom of the loss of exaltation and affective power (as discussed in the preceding chapter). Dorothy Thompson has written, "Apart from musical accompaniment, this matter of beat, cadence, the rise and fall of sentences, is part of the magic of poetry and prose, contributing to its evocative characters, its overtones and undertones, its symphonic style, which greatly distinguishes the [King James] Bible."[2]

SUMMARY

Good rhythm is one of the most immediately discernible excellences in the KJV and its modern heirs, while halting and staccato rhythm is one of the most obvious infelicities of modernizing translations. In both prose and poetry, the ESV "delivers the goods" in its flow of language. The benefits of fluency are one of the rewards that come to people who choose the ESV.

14

THE ENGLISH STANDARD VERSION
AS A LITERARY BIBLE

In its external format, the Bible is a literary anthology. This means that a host of literary genres make up most of the Bible. Additionally, the style of writing only occasionally resembles the kind of expository prose that we use to transact the basic business of life. Literature advertises its difference from everyday spoken discourse. An English Bible is adequate only if it captures the literary quality of the original.

Half of my teaching and publishing career has been devoted to the Bible as literature. From time to time I have pondered what effect it would have had on my career not to have the Revised Standard Version and more recently the English Standard Version (ESV) as a translation. My conclusion is always the same: I could not have had a flourishing career in the Bible as literature if the only modern versions at my disposal had been the New International Version (NIV) and the New American Standard Bible (NASB). Of course, dynamic equivalent translations would not have yielded a Bible-as-literature career at all.

In chapter 6 I explored the ways in which the King James Version (KJV) is preeminent among English Bible translations for its literary qualities. My task in this chapter is to demonstrate the high degree to which the ESV retains the literary excellence of the KJV and its sixteenth-century predecessors.

Concrete Diction

The ever-present motto in writing and literature classrooms is that the task of literature is to "show rather than tell." To show means to embody experience and reality and ideas in concrete actions, characters, and things. To tell means to use abstraction and explanation and assertion rather than embodiment. It is no exaggeration to say that English Bible translations fall decisively into one of the two camps I have just described.

Dynamic equivalent translations move inevitably in the direction of abstraction and commentary. This is the case because to render something concretely involves indirection and therefore produces a statement that requires interpretation. It makes a Bible reader continuously pause to figure out what something means. Dynamic equivalence, by contrast, is based on the premise of Spelling It Out.

If we believe that God gave us the Bible that he wishes us to have, the decisions of Bible translators are easy: all they need to do is reproduce in English what the original authors wrote. But if a target audience rather than the original text calls the shots, translators are at pains to replace what in the original text is concrete with something explanatory and therefore abstract.

The ESV meets the literary criterion of concrete diction. This is guaranteed by its "essentially literal" philosophy based on the principle of verbal equivalence. Below are a few examples, heightened by being contrasted to dynamic equivalent versions of the same passages.

I start with the most egregious imposition of abstraction in the annals of English Bible translation, namely, the NIV rendition of Ecclesiastes 1:2: "Meaningless! Meaningless!" The scholarly consensus is that the Hebrew word thus translated means vapor or breath, as the ESV note asserts. Most English translations follow the KJV in translating the verse "vanity of vanities" (RSV, NASB, NKJV, JB, ESV). This preserves some of the literary ambiguity of the image. But other dynamic equivalent translations agree with the NIV impulse toward abstraction: "emptiness, emptiness" (NEB); "futility, utter futility" (REB); "Nothing makes sense! Everything is nonsense" (CEV).

To use concrete language is to cast one's lot with particularity as opposed to generality and vagueness. Scholars of Hebrew and Greek agree with the verdict of John Livingston Lowes that in the Hebrew language of the Old Testament "the vocabulary was consciously pictorial and concrete in its character," and that "the writers of the Old Testament—and to a less degree those of the New as well—thought and felt and spoke in images."[1]

The ESV preserves this quality of the original Bible. It speaks of Egypt as the "house" of slavery, not the more generalized "land" of slavery (NIV, NEB, REB). It retains the particularity of God's edict to Adam (Gen. 2:17) that "in the day" he eats of the forbidden fruit he will die, not the vague "when you eat of it" (NIV). In the ESV Samuel's execution of Agag comes alive as we read that Samuel "hacked Agag to pieces before the Lord" (1 Sam. 15:33), but we cease to picture anything when particularity gives way to abstraction: "And Samuel put Agag to death before the Lord" (NIV). The Old Testament prophets were poets at heart in the way they spoke and wrote. Thus Ezekiel claims that the house of Israel had "a hard forehead and a stubborn heart" (Ezek. 3:7, ESV). Translators who believe that "hard forehead" is too difficult for their target audience arrive on the scene with abstractions such as "hardened and obstinate" (NIV), "stubborn and obstinate" (NASB), and "stubborn and defiant" (GNB).

Another ploy of dynamic equivalent translators is to add commentary to the concretion of the original, so that we end up with a hybrid blend of what the biblical author actually wrote and abstract commentary added by the translators. Of course an English reader has no clue that this has happened. In Psalm 73:2 the poet writes, "my steps had nearly slipped" (ESV). This is nicely concrete and multiple in its meanings. But it requires a reader to ponder how spiritual doubt is like slipping while walking. So some translation committees add commentary to the translation. In the following examples, I have italicized the commentary to show what was added:

- "My feet were slipping, *and I was almost gone*" (NLT).
- "But I almost stumbled *and fell*" (CEV).
- "I had almost *lost my faith*" (NCV).
- "*My faith* was almost *gone*" (GNB).

At the heart of the dynamic equivalent venture is the premise that the biblical text is often inadequate and in need of improvement, and a move toward abstraction is often regarded as an improvement.

While individual moves from concreteness to abstraction might seem insignificant, when multiplied over the entire Bible it produces a very different book from the original text. Paul speaks of "a wide door" that has opened up for him (1 Cor. 16:9, ESV). In the NIV the pictorial "wide" becomes the vague "great." Other dynamic equivalent translations push the statement even further in the direction of abstraction: "a good opportunity" (NCV); "a wonderful opportunity" (CEV); "a real opportunity" (GNB). The "wide door" has fled the scene.

Retaining Figurative Language

A major dimension of literature is figurative language. Poetry, of course, relies almost entirely on figurative language. But every part of the Bible is saturated with figurative language, including the discourses of Jesus, the New Testament epistles, and the book of Revelation. Some English translations do a conscientious job of retaining figurative language, while dynamic equivalent translators often can't wait to remove the figures of speech because their target audience allegedly finds figurative language too difficult to negotiate. Of course this immediately violates the intention of the original authors.

Psalm 1:1 became a celebrated example not only because the Good News Bible eliminated the metaphors, but also because Eugene Nida, the founder of dynamic equivalence, gave an explanation of why it was good to have removed the metaphors of the original. In the ESV Psalm 1:1 is the very touchstone of figurative language:

> Blessed is the man
> > who walks not in the counsel of the wicked,
> nor stands in the way of sinners,
> > nor sits in the seat of scoffers.

Walks, stands, sits in the seat: each of these metaphors embodies a distinct piece of information about aligning oneself with "the wicked," and as a series they form a sequence of increasing immersion in evil. That poetic richness evaporates in the rendition of the Good News Bible:

> Happy are those
> > who reject the advice of evil men,
> > who do not follow the example of sinners
> > or join those who have no use for God.

Here we lose not only the vividness of the imagery but also the multiplicity of meanings that the metaphors contain.

Why would translators wish to remove the metaphor that the Holy Spirit prompted the poet to invent? Eugene Nida speaks for the whole family of dynamic equivalence translators. Figurative language such as we find in Psalm 1:1 seems "strange" to "many present-day readers," with the result that removing the metaphors makes the verse "so much clearer."[2] The introduction to the NLT agrees: "Metaphorical language is sometimes difficult for contemporary readers to understand, so at times we have chosen to . . . illuminate the meaning of a metaphor." I will note in passing that the references to modern readers in those two quotations are a common maneuver of dynamic equivalence advocates. According to this argument, modern readers, with the most sophisticated education in the history of the human race, are grossly inferior to the original readers of the Bible and need help that the original readers did not.

The ESV can be trusted to preserve the figurative language of the original authors. This is how to respect the authorial intention of the writers. If Luke 11:20 speaks of "the finger of God," that is what the ESV delivers, not the substitute abstraction "power" of God (CEV, GNB, NCV). If Job is reported to have said, "I will teach you concerning the hand of God" (Job 27:11), that is what we will find in the ESV, not replacements such as "the power of God" (NIV) or "God's power" (multiple dynamic equivalent translations).

STYLISTIC VARIETY

The Bible is nearly as varied as a literary anthology such as *The Norton Anthology of English Literature*. To retain as much of that variety as possible is not simply to indulge a literary taste. It is instead to remain faithful to what the biblical authors wrote and to their intentions regarding what they wrote.

The stylistic variety of the Bible is on a collision course with a translation philosophy that believes translators should be governed by what they assume to be the reading and theological abilities of their target audience. The target audience envisioned by dynamic equivalent translators has such low linguistic and comprehension ability that there is no scope for stylistic variety to find its way into the translation. Everything is flattened out to a monotone style. Not so with the ESV.

At the beginning of most of the New Testament epistles we find an ingredient that Christian writers added to the Greco-Roman epistolary template. Called a thanksgiving, it is so exalted and uplifting that it ranks as among the most exhilarating genres in the whole Bible. It is accordingly a touchstone of high style in the Bible. Obviously an epistolary thanksgiving should not sound like straightforward informational writing. In the ESV it does not sound that way, as illustrated by an excerpt from the thanksgiving in the letter to the Ephesians: "In him we have redemption through his blood, the forgiveness of our trespasses, according to the riches of his grace, which he lavished upon us, in all wisdom and insight making known to us the mystery of his will, according to his purpose, which he set forth in Christ as a plan for the fullness of time, to unite all things in him, things in heaven and things on earth" (Eph. 1:7–10). Literary scholars call this a prose poem, fired by a lyric exuberance in which the words and feelings and ideas tumble onto the page. The flowing syntax is an important part of the passage (and I note in this regard that the entire quotation is a single sentence).

In most dynamic equivalent translations, the syntax and vocabulary of the passage are scaled down until the passage resembles pretty much any other genre in the Bible. Here is an example:

> He is so rich in kindness and grace that he purchased our freedom with the blood of his Son and forgave our sins. He has showered his kindness on us, along with all wisdom and understanding.
>
> God has now revealed to us his mysterious plan regarding Christ, a plan to fulfill his own good pleasure. And this is the plan: At the right time he will bring everything together under the authority of Christ—everything in heaven and on earth. (NLT)

The distinctiveness that the passage should possess has been merged into the uniform style of the Bible as a whole designed for a sixth-grade reader.

One of the fallacies foisted on the public is that the King James Bible and the ESV are written in a uniformly high style. They are not. Many of the narratives in the ESV are written in a beautifully simple style: "In those days a decree went out from Caesar Augustus that all the world should be registered. This was the first registration when Quirinius was governor of Syria. And all went to be registered, each to his own town. And Joseph also went up from Galilee, from the town of Nazareth, to Judea, to the city of David, which is called Bethlehem" (Luke 2:1–4). This is a more beautiful pitch than that of the daily newspaper, but the eloquence that we feel as we read or hear the passage is an eloquence of simplicity.

When translators simply follow the contours of what the biblical authors wrote, prophetic visionary writing will *sound* like visionary writing, not like an interdepartmental communiqué:

> "Behold, the days are coming," declares the LORD,
> "when the plowman shall overtake the reaper
> and the treader of grapes him who sows the seed."
>   (Amos 9:13, ESV)

The CEV manages to make the vision sound like a bulletin from the Department of Agriculture:

You will have such a harvest
that you won't be able
to bring in all of your wheat
before plowing time.
You will have grapes left over
from season to season.

A lot of damage was done to English Bible translation when the concept of a target audience became enthroned.

What about the proverbs of the Bible? Don't they inevitably retain their aphoristic flavor in all English translations? Unfortunately the answer is no. The ESV managed to retain most of the aphoristic sparkle of the KJV:

- "Better is the end of a thing than its beginning" (Eccles. 7:8).
- "A soft answer turns away wrath" (Prov. 15:1).
- "Hope deferred makes the heart sick" (Prov. 13:12).
- "Do not neglect to show hospitality to strangers, for thereby some have entertained angels unawares" (Heb. 13:2).
- "His divine power has granted to us all things that pertain to life and godliness" (2 Pet. 1:3).

If we ask how these memorable proverbs can be rendered in prosaic manner, we do not need to look far:

- "Finishing is better than starting" (NLT).
- "A gentle answer will calm a person's anger" (NCV).
- "Not getting what you want / can make you feel sick" (CEV).
- "Don't neglect to show hospitality, for by doing this some have welcomed angels as guests without knowing it" (HCSB).
- "Jesus has the power of God, by which he has given us everything we need to live and to serve God" (NCV).

153

Of course it is not the *intention* of those who produce modernizing translations to destroy the literary integrity of the Bible, but that is the *effect* because the translators did not deliberately set out to *preserve* the literary quality of the Bible.

Why It Matters That the ESV Is a Literary Bible

There are at least four huge ramifications in regard to whether or not a Bible translation preserves the literary qualities of the original text. It is untrue that a literary Bible is the optional indulgence of a coterie of literary enthusiasts. It is a requirement, not an elective.

We can begin with the cornerstone of modern evangelical hermeneutics—authorial intention. This hermeneutical principle means that an interpretation of a biblical text—and by extension the translation of it from the original—must be based on what the author of the text intended. It should be obvious that when the writers of the Bible enshrined their utterances in literary forms, they *intended* their writings to be handled as literary documents. A translation that retains the literary nature of the Bible respects this authorial intention, while translations that do not retain the literary quality of the Bible violate authorial intention.

Second, literature as a form of discourse communicates at a richer level than does nonliterary writing. Francis Schaeffer correctly remarked that "art forms add strength" to an utterance and that "we can count on [it]" that the presence of artistry will "heighten the impact" of a piece of writing.[3] One reason the Bible is in eclipse in evangelical churches is that the translations used in many churches lack the splendor and authority that would inspire obedience or even interest. English Bibles that sound like the buzz at the corner shop or like the company newsletter are given the weight and credence of those genres.

Third, there is an aesthetic dimension to a literary Bible. The Bible itself makes it clear that God is the source of beauty and that he values it. The writer of Ecclesiastes states flat out what his theory of writing is, and his statement is an artistic credo. He not only "wrote words of truth" but also "sought to find words of delight" (Eccles. 12:10, ESV). "Words of delight": this writer was a wordsmith in a quest for beauty of expression. It is not saying too much that prosaic translations signal their indifference to aesthetic criteria by the way they translate the phrase *words of delight*. Prosaic translations render it "just the right words" (multiple translations) and "I tried to explain these things in the best and most accurate way" (CEV)—in other words, strictly utilitarian, expository, textbook prose, without any admixture of literary beauty and the accompanying quality of mystery.

Finally, literature tends toward multilayered meanings. The literary term for this is *ambiguity*—saying more than one thing at the same time. Of course this places greater interpretive demands on a reader. Literary translators view this as (1) a merit and (2) God's intention in the Bible (inasmuch as he moved the authors to write literature). Literary Bibles tend toward multilayered fullness, while dynamic equivalent translations are often one-dimensional. They repeatedly narrow down the possible meanings to just one. When Psalm 91:1 gives us the metaphor of a person "who dwells in the shelter of the Most High" (ESV and others), the image of dwelling in a house yields multiple meanings. One-dimensional translations narrow those meanings to one: "under the protection of" (CEV); "whoever goes to the LORD for safety" (GNB); "those who go to God Most High for safety" (NCV).

SUMMARY

Literary scholars are not the people who have put the literary nature of the Bible "on the table." The authors of the Bible themselves put

155

the topic on the agenda of important topics for Bible translators and readers. To ignore the literary aspects of the Bible is to disregard authorial intention and distort the kind of book the Bible is. The KJV brought to a climax the process of literary refinement that had occurred through a succession of translations throughout the sixteenth century. By remaining faithful to this tradition, the ESV is as literary as a modern Bible can be while remaining true to the original Bible.

CONCLUSION

Why You Can Trust the English Standard Version

The burden of the preceding chapters has been to show the close connection between the English Standard Version (ESV) and the Tyndale–King James tradition. By showing that link, I have made an implicit defense of the ESV as a superior translation. In my conclusion I will make that claim even more directly. I have assembled a slate of twelve reasons why you can trust the ESV as your English Bible.

1. KEEPING TO THE ESSENTIAL TASK OF TRANSLATION

You can trust the ESV to keep to the essential task of translation, namely, translation.

English Bible translation took a wrong turn when translators became arrogant in regard to how much they were free to do with the biblical text. A cluster of factors fed into this, including a lowered respect for the rights of biblical authors to be allowed to say what they say, an exaggerated deference to what the translators assumed their readers to be and want, and a view of translation that included license to do a range of things beyond translation of words from the Hebrew and Greek biblical texts into English. In short, dynamic equivalent translators feel free to add the roles of editor, exegete, and commentator to their role of translator.

The ESV committee did not enlarge its job description in these ways. The translators did not become editors who reduced the language and syntax of the biblical authors to match a modern reader with assumed low reading ability. They did not use the editorial prerogative of changing gender references. The ESV shows no signs of the nervousness of dynamic equivalent translators over the possibility that ignorant readers are incapable of handling anything that might require thought or research as a prerequisite to understanding. The result is obvious: you can be confident that what is in the ESV is neither more nor less than an English rendition of the words of the biblical authors.

2. TRANSPARENCY TO THE ORIGINAL

Except where a completely literal translation would have been unintelligible to an English reader, you can trust the ESV to be transparent to the original text.

An essentially literal translation does not insert an intermediary layer of interpretation between the reader and the original text. When on extremely rare occasions the ESV contains something other than an English equivalent of the actual words used by a biblical author, it gives you an accompanying note that gives the literal rendering. In this and other ways, you can trust the ESV to keep the record clear.

I myself can conceive of no other reason for translation than that it brings a reader as close to the original text as the process of translation allows. Surely we want to know what the author actually wrote, and in fact we ourselves would object if a publisher changed what we had written and then attributed it to us.

Transparency to the original text of the Bible needs to be differentiated from the kind of transparency that dynamic equivalent translators advocate. The goal with modernizing translations is to make everything immediately understandable—transparent—to a modern reader. The ESV seeks to take a reader directly to what the biblical authors wrote. If the picture of Job's prosperity in Job 36:16 includes the detail that "what was set on [his] table was full of fatness," that is what the ESV gives you, not replacements such as "the best food" (NLT 1996) or "a generous table" (REB).

3. Preserving the Full Interpretive Potential of the Original

You can trust the ESV to preserve the full interpretive potential of the original text.

The ESV resists the following common forms of reductionism that afflict dynamic equivalent translations:

- simplifying the original text to a lowest common denominator of contemporary readers
- choosing just one of the potential meanings of a passage and putting only that in front of the reader
- making preemptive interpretive strikes so as to prevent the reader from making interpretive decisions for himself or herself
- eliminating technical or difficult theological vocabulary and substituting nontechnical vocabulary
- interpreting figurative language right in the translation
- assuming that modern readers are inferior to both the original audience of the Bible and readers of the English Bible through the centuries
- reducing the level of vocabulary
- diminishing the literary beauty and exaltation of the Bible
- paring down the affective power of the Bible
- reducing the stylistic variety of the original text to a monotone arrived at by slanting the translation toward a target audience with allegedly low linguistic and cognitive abilities

Stated positively, you can trust the ESV to do the following things as a way of preserving the full richness and exegetical potential of the Bible:

- presenting language as beautiful and sophisticated as the original itself possesses
- embodying as many levels of meaning as the original contains
- retaining poetry in its original, literal expression
- reproducing the stylistic range of the original
- giving readers theological terminology as complex as the original contains

The goal of an essentially literal translation like the ESV is fullness. The effect of dynamic equivalent translations has been diminishment—diminishment in the form of reduced expectations of Bible readers, reduced respect for biblical authors, impoverishment of language, emaciated theology, a one-dimensional Bible in regard to legitimate multiple meanings, and lowered literary standards.

4. NOT MIXING COMMENTARY WITH TRANSLATION

You can trust the ESV not to mislead you regarding where translation of the original ends and commentary from the translators begins.

We normally operate on the premise that the book that a publisher puts into our hands is what the original author actually wrote. Within the necessary changes that all translation requires, an essentially literal translation such as the ESV does not betray that trust. It keeps to an absolute minimum the intermingling of interpretive commentary with translation. An essentially literal translation operates on the premise that a translator is a steward of what someone else has written, not an editor and exegete who needs to correct what someone else has written.

The ESV does not contain an overlay of commentary designed to explain things that the original text does not spell out. The ESV translators believe that a phrase of Psalm 23:2 is beautiful and adequate as it is in the original: "He leads me beside still waters." They feel no need to Spell It Out by adding the additional commentary "where I may rest" (REB). Bible study groups using the ESV do not need to cope with members' contributions based on material that is not in the original text (something that happens incessantly with dynamic equivalent translations).

5. Preserving Theological Precision

You can trust the ESV to preserve theological precision.

At the heart of dynamic equivalence is uneasiness about theological vocabulary. This is partly fueled by the dynamic equivalent common assumption that the Bible should "not sound like the Bible" (that is, like familiar translations in the KJV tradition) and partly by a view of the target audience as theologically uneducated and/or uninterested in theology. A typical statement is the statement in the preface to the CEV that the translation is committed to "avoidance of traditionally theological language and biblical words."

The ESV translation committee believes to the contrary that we cannot build an adequate theology without an adequate theological vocabulary. A theological concept of justification can be built on the statement (Rom. 3:24) that we "are justified by his grace as a gift" (ESV), but not on dynamic equivalent paraphrases such as we "are put right with [God]" (GNB); "God in his gracious kindness declares us not guilty" (NLT 1996); and "God treats us much better than we deserve" (CEV). You can trust the ESV to use the word *propitiation* when it appears in the original (Rom. 3:25; Heb. 2:17; 1 John 2:2; 1 John 4:10). In this regard I recall hearing a member of the NIV translation committee claim that "propitiation is exactly the right word, but we cannot use it because people do not know

161

what it means." The ESV assumes that people can be educated to understand what God inspired the biblical authors to write.

6. Not Needing to Correct the Translation in Preaching and Teaching

You can trust the ESV to spare an expository preacher or teacher from needing to correct the biblical text.

One reason for the decline in expository preaching and inductive Bible study is that, in the wake of the dynamic equivalent revolution, English translations of the Bible consistently need to be corrected from the pulpit and in small group Bible studies. It is impossible to conduct a close reading of an unreliable text. You can trust an essentially literal translation largely to eliminate the need to resort to the formula "now what the original actually says is . . ." Expository preacher John Piper said in an address that he "can't preach from a dynamic equivalent Bible," because it does not give him the text of the biblical authors.

7. Preserving What the Biblical Writers Actually Wrote

You can trust the ESV not to "improve" the Bible by resolving all interpretive difficulties in the direction of what a given translation committee decides to parcel out to its readers.

At the heart of essentially literal Bible translation is the conviction that God gave us the Bible that he wants us to have. At the heart of the dynamic equivalence enterprise is the conviction that the Bible needs continuous correction and improvement. These two viewpoints cannot be reconciled.

A related disagreement between the rival translation philosophies is whether or not translators should massage the biblical text to remove all difficulties and obscurities that the text contains.

The starting premise of dynamic equivalence is that everything in the Bible should be immediately understandable to a reader. As a result, dynamic equivalence translations conduct continuous preemptive interpretive strikes about which readers do not have a clue.

You can expect the ESV to pass on interpretive difficulties to the reader. Is this a virtue? It is. The goal is to know what the original authors said. If they passed difficulties on to *their* readers, translators need to do the same. If Mark 9:50 says, "Have salt in yourselves," that is what you will find in the ESV, even though it is an enigmatic command.

8. PRESERVING THE LITERARY QUALITIES OF THE BIBLE

You can trust the ESV to preserve the literary qualities of the Bible.

The Bible in its original is a very literary book. Some translators are determined to preserve the literary qualities of the Bible, and some are not. For the ESV translation committee, producing a literary Bible came automatically and did not require a conscious choice. This is because the starting point of the ESV was the Revised Standard Version, which in turn is the closest modern approximation to the King James Version (KJV). Under those circumstances, it would have taken a conscious effort *not* to produce a literary Bible.

Although the following position was not officially adopted by the ESV translators, it represents the assumption with which the ESV was forged. The position is this: if we believe that the Holy Spirit inspired the authors of the Bible to write as they did, it was ultimately the Holy Spirit who gave us a literary Bible. It was the Holy Spirit who gave us figurative language, and an essentially literal translation preserves that figurative language.

163

9. PRESERVING THE DIGNITY AND BEAUTY OF THE BIBLE

You can trust the ESV to preserve the exaltation, dignity, and beauty of the Bible.

It will be apparent that the generalizations that I develop in this conclusion underscore the thesis of my entire book, namely, that the greatness of the ESV is a result of its being positioned in the King James tradition. The language of the KJV is matchless, and the ESV (with the RSV as intermediary) preserves the qualities of the KJV in a modern idiom.

Every English Bible translation has two dimensions—content and form. When we apply this twofold grid to modernizing translations, we find that the scene is more complex than the umbrella "dynamic equivalence" covers. At the level of *content*, the essential issue is, indeed, dynamic equivalence. But that label is largely useless to describe what modernizing translations do at the level of vocabulary and style.

Here the important principle is the desire to produce a colloquial Bible that reproduces the informality of contemporary discourse. But not *all* contemporary discourse. In fact, the prefaces and other documents in which modernizing translators explain what they have done is expressed in a highly formal and sophisticated style of writing. This results in the strange situation of translators who do not really believe what they say about modern readers and about the adequacy of sixth-grade vocabulary to convey truth.

The effect of the colloquial translations is to diminish dignity and beauty of expression. The ESV champions dignity, exaltation, and beauty. In the ESV you can expect to read, "Behold, I stand at the door and knock" (Rev. 3:20, KJV, NASB, ESV). In the ESV you will find the awe-inspiring lead-in, "Truly, truly, I say to you," not a translation that has scaled the voltage down to "I tell you the truth" (NIV, NLT) or "I tell you for certain" (CEV). In the ESV the beloved in Song of Solomon 2:4 will be brought "to the banqueting house," not to a "special large room for eating," and the beloved will attest that "his banner over me was love," not that "it's obvious how much he loves me" (NLV).

10. BEING CONSISTENT WITH THE DOCTRINE OF INSPIRATION

You can trust the ESV to adhere to the doctrine of plenary or verbal inspiration.

The ESV is based on the premise that the very words of the Bible are inspired and therefore inviolable. Another way of saying this is that an essentially literal translation like the ESV will not lead people unwittingly to violate the very principle of verbal inspiration that they theoretically endorse. Throughout the Bible, Scripture is referred to as the word of God, not the thought(s) of God. Jesus himself said that "*the words* that I have spoken to you are spirit and life" (John 6:63, ESV; italics added).

The adherence of dynamic equivalent translators to plenary or verbal inspiration is lip service. In actual practice these translators feel totally free to dispense with the actual words of Scripture. From that premise, who cares that Psalm 141:3 says "set a guard . . . over my mouth"? Dynamic equivalent translators do not believe that the words *guard* and *mouth* are inviolable because they are inspired. In this view it is *the thought* that is inspired, so there is nothing to prevent the translators from changing the statement to read, "Take control of what I say" (NLT). It cannot be stated too often that the biblical authors had the resources to say something the way dynamic equivalent translators render it, and they did not do so. Dynamic equivalent translators are not supplying something that the biblical authors lacked; they are changing what the biblical authors wrote.

11. PROVIDING EQUIVALENCE RATHER THAN REPLACEMENT OR SUBSTITUTION

You can trust the ESV not to substitute something for what the biblical authors actually wrote.

I noted earlier in this book that the formula *dynamic equivalence* is a misleading label for what we actually find in these translations. Sometimes, it is true, the word *equivalence* is accurate. To change the word *mouth* to *tongue* (NCV) in Psalm 141:3 is an example of equivalence. But in the majority of changes to the original biblical text, so-called dynamic equivalent translations give us a replacement or substitute of what is in the original, not an equivalent or correspondence. When the literal "firstfruits" (James 1:18) is rendered as "crown" (MESSAGE) or "prized possession" (NLT), we have been given a substitution and replacement. Because the ESV is an essentially literal translation, you can trust it not to give you a substitute Bible.

12. SHOWING RESPECT FOR BIBLICAL AUTHORS AND READERS

You can trust the ESV not to be condescending to biblical authors and readers.

We do not need to read very far in the prefaces to dynamic equivalent translations to pick up an attitude of extreme condescension toward biblical authors and readers. As for the biblical authors, they need continuously to be corrected and improved. What they wrote cannot possibly be correct or adequate for modern English readers. They gave us metaphors, and we know that many of these are beyond modern comprehension. The biblical authors were ambiguous or difficult; shame on them—they should have done better. So runs the argument.

As for the biblical readers presupposed by dynamic equivalent translations, they are a hopeless lot. They have not moved beyond

166

a grade-school level of linguistic skill or comprehension. There are things in the Bible that "have little meaning" for "most readers today" (NIV preface), or that seem "strange" to "many present-day readers" (Eugene Nida on the metaphors in Psalm 1:1). Furthermore, it is assumed that readers cannot be educated to understand these things.

The ESV committee refuses to believe that biblical authors and readers are inept. The writers of the Bible are assumed to be in command of their writing. They didn't *try to say* something; they said it. The ESV committee does not presume to know what biblical authors meant beyond what they wrote; we can trust that what the authors wrote is what they meant.

Similarly with Bible readers. They are people of normal intelligence. They can rise above a grade-school level of language and thinking. They can be educated in theological concepts and terms. They can rise above the spoken idiom of the coffee shop and neighborhood chat. They have an aesthetic sense that welcomes beauty and dignity of expression. They should not be asked to leave adult thinking and ways of speaking at the door when they come to read the Bible.

CONCLUSION

English Bible translation stands at a watershed moment. For half a century, dynamic equivalence has been the guiding translation philosophy behind most new translations. Each successive wave of these translations has tended to be increasingly bold in departing from the words of the original text. Stated another way, we can trace an arc of increasingly aggressive changing, adding to, and subtracting from the words that the biblical authors wrote. Modernizing translations are a carefully orchestrated exercise (which I experience as a conspiracy) to prevent readers from knowing what the biblical authors actually wrote.

The issues that are at stake in the current debate about Bible translation are immense. Boiled down to its essence, what is at stake is whether English Bible readers will have the Word of God or a mixture of God's Word with human commentary and interpretation—the Bible as it really is or a substitute Bible.

NOTES

Chapter One: The Translations That Make up the Tradition

1. H. W. Hoare, *The Evolution of the English Bible* (New York: E. P. Dutton, 1901), 82.

2. David Daniell, *The Bible in English: Its History and Influence* (New Haven, CT: Yale University Press, 2003), 66.

3. Alec Gilmore, *A Dictionary of the English Bible and Its Origins* (Sheffield, UK: Sheffield Academic Press, 2000), 186.

4. Daniell, *The Bible in English,* 158.

5. Ibid.

6. Donald L. Brake, *A Visual History of the English Bible* (Grand Rapids, MI: Baker Books, 2008), 106.

7. John Foxe, *Foxe's Book of Martyrs* (Peabody, MA: Hendrickson, 2004), 225.

8. Charles C. Butterworth, *The Literary Lineage of the King James Bible, 1340–1611* (Philadelphia: University of Pennsylvania Press, 1941), 242.

9. Geddes MacGregor, *The Bible in the Making* (Philadelphia: J. B. Lippincott, 1959), 181.

10. Leland Ryken, *The Legacy of the King James Bible* (Wheaton, IL: Crossway, 2011).

Chapter Two: How the Bible Was Viewed

1. John Strype, *Memorials of the Most Reverend Father in God Thomas Cranmer* (London: George Routledge, 1853), 1:92.

2. A brief survey of Puritan and Reformed views of inspiration can be found in Philip Edgcumbe Hughes, "The Inspiration of Scripture in the English Reformers Illuminated by John Calvin," *Westminster Theological Journal* 23 (1961): 129–50; also in B. B. Warfield, *The Westminster Assembly and Its Work* (New York: Oxford University Press, 1931), 261–333.

3. John Purvey, Prologue to the Wyclif Bible, chap. 15, trans. Michael Marlowe, http://www.bible-researcher.com/wyclif2.html.

4. Quoted in David Norton, *A History of the Bible as Literature* (Cambridge: Cambridge University Press, 1993), 1:81.

Chapter Three: Principles of Translation

1. James Andrew Clark, "Hidden Tyndale in *OED*'s First Instances from Miles Coverdale's 1535 Bible," *Notes and Queries* 45 (1998): 289–93.

2. William Tyndale, Preface to *The Obedience of a Christian Man*, quoted in David Norton, *A History of the Bible as Literature* (Cambridge: Cambridge University Press, 1993), 1:98.

3. Alister McGrath, *In the Beginning: The Story of the King James Bible and How It Changed a Nation, a Language, and a Culture* (New York: Anchor Books, 2001), 250.

4. Ibid., 252.

5. John Purvey, Prologue to the Wyclif Bible, chap. 15, trans. Michael Marlowe, http://www.bible-researcher.com/wyclif2.html.

6. Anne Hudson, ed., *Selections from English Wycliffite Writings* (Cambridge: Cambridge University Press, 1978), 174–75.

7. David Daniell, *William Tyndale: A Biography* (New Haven, CT: Yale University Press, 1994), 120.

Chapter Four: Language and Style

1. Benson Bobrick, *Wide as the Waters: The Story of the English Bible and the Revolution It Inspired* (New York: Penguin, 2002), 254; Alister McGrath, *In the Beginning: The Story of the King James Bible and How It Changed a Nation, a Language, and a Culture* (New York: Anchor Books, 2001), 262.

2. Northrop Frye, *The Great Code: The Bible and Literature* (New York: Harcourt Brace Jovanovich, 1982), 211.

3. Donald Coggan, *The English Bible* (London: Longmans, Green, 1963), 23.

4. John Livingston Lowes, "The Noblest Monument of English Prose," in *Essays in Appreciation* (Boston: Houghton Mifflin, 1936), 15.

5. David Daniell, *The Bible in English: Its History and Influence* (New Haven, CT: Yale University Press, 2003), 429.

6. Charles Dinsmore, *The English Bible as Literature* (Boston: Houghton Mifflin, 1931), 92.

7. Charles C. Butterworth, *The Literary Lineage of the King James Bible, 1340–1611* (Philadelphia: University of Pennsylvania Press, 1941), 1.

Chapter Five: Rhythm and Oral Effects

1. John Seldon, *Table Talk*, as quoted in Adam Nicolson, *God's Secretaries: The Making of the King James Bible* (New York: HarperCollins, 2003), 209.

2. Ibid.

3. Eugene A. Nida and Charles R. Taber, *The Theory and Practice of Translation* (Leiden: E. J. Brill, 1969), 13.

4. Lane Cooper, *Certain Rhythms in the English Bible* (Ithaca, NY: Cornell University Press, 1952).

5. Craig Thompson, *The Bible in English, 1525–1611* (Ithaca, NY: Cornell University Press, 1958), 17.

Chapter Six: A Literary Bible

1. Alister McGrath, *In the Beginning: The Story of the King James Bible and How It Changed a Nation, a Language, and a Culture* (New York: Anchor Books, 2001), 254–55.

2. For elaboration of why it is not surprising that the King James translators produced a literary Bible, see Leland Ryken, *The Legacy of the King James Bible* (Wheaton, IL: Crossway, 2011), 124–27.

3. Reynolds Price, *Three Gospels* (New York: Scribner, 1996), 23.

4. Albert S. Cook, "The 'Authorized Version' and Its Influence," in *The Cambridge History of English Literature* (Cambridge: Cambridge University Press, 1933), 4:22–23.

5. C. Boyd McAfee, *The Greatest English Classic* (New York: Harper and Brothers, 1912), 104.

6. John Livingston Lowes, "The Noblest Monument of English Prose," in *Essays in Appreciation* (Boston: Houghton Mifflin, 1936), 7, 9.

7. J. R. R. Tolkien, "On Fairy-Stories," in *Essays Presented to Charles Williams*, ed. C. S. Lewis (1947; repr. Grand Rapids, MI: Eerdmans, 1966), 67.

8. David Daniell, *The Bible in English: Its History and Influence* (New Haven, CT: Yale University Press, 2003), 158.

9. Charles Dinsmore, *The English Bible as Literature* (Boston: Houghton Mifflin, 1931), 92.

Chapter Seven: A Unified Tradition

1. Eugene Peterson, *Eat This Book: A Conversation in the Art of Spiritual Reading* (Grand Rapids, MI: Eerdmans, 2006), 162.

2. In the preface to his Greek New Testament (1516), Erasmus writes: "Christ wishes His mysteries published as openly as possible. I would even . . . the farmer sing some portion of them at the plow." Desiderius Erasmus, *Christian Humanism and the Reformation: Selected Writings,* ed. John C. Olin (New York: Harper 1965), 97.

3. C. L. Wrenn, review of NEB in *Studia Evangelica,* in *The New English Bible Reviewed*, ed. Dennis Nineham (London: Epworth, 1965), 138.

4. William Tyndale, Preface to 1526 New Testament, quoted in David Daniell, *William Tyndale: A Biography* (New Haven, CT: Yale University Press, 1994), 145–46. Also accessible at http://www.bible-researcher.com/tyndale2.html.

5. Adam Nicolson, *God's Secretaries: The Making of the King James Bible* (New York: HarperCollins, 2003), 223.

6. Alister McGrath, *In the Beginning: The Story of the King James Bible and How It Changed a Nation, a Language, and a Culture* (New York: Anchor Books, 2001), 176–78.

7. John Livingston Lowes, "The Noblest Monument of English Prose," in *Essays in Appreciation* (Boston: Houghton Mifflin, 1936), 22–23.

8. Benson Bobrick, *Wide as the Waters: The Story of the English Bible and the Revolution It Inspired* (New York: Penguin, 2001), 239–40, 158.

9. Craig R. Thompson, *The Bible in English, 1525–1611* (Ithaca, NY: Cornell University Press, 1958), 27.

10. Charles C. Butterworth, *The Literary Lineage of the King James Bible, 1340–1611* (Philadelphia: University of Pennsylvania Press, 1941), 242.

Chapter Eight: Modern Translation at the Crossroads

1. William A. Irwin, "Method and Procedure in the Revision," in *An Introduction to the Revised Standard Version of the Old Testament*, ed. Luther A. Weigle (New York: Nelson, 1952), 13–14.

2. Eugene Nida, interviewed by David Neff, "Meaning-full Translations," *Christianity Today*, October 7, 2002, 46–49.

3. Calvin Linton, "The Importance of Literary Style," in *The Making of the NIV*, ed. Kenneth L. Barker (Grand Rapids, MI: Baker Books, 1991), 26.

4. Edwin H. Palmer, quoted in D. A. Carson, *The King James Version Debate: A Plea for Realism* (Grand Rapids, MI: Baker Books, 1979), 102.

5. Eugene Peterson, *Eat This Book: A Conversation in the Art of Spiritual Reading* (Grand Rapids, MI: Eerdmans, 2006), 162–63.

Chapter Nine: What Reviewers Say about Modernizing Translations

1. James Andrew Clark, "Hidden Tyndale in *OED*'s First Instances from Miles Coverdale's 1535 Bible," *Notes and Queries* 45 (1998): 289–93.

2. Henry Gifford, review of NEB, in *The New English Bible Reviewed*, ed. David Nineham (London: Epworth, 1965), 111. Originally published in *Essays in Criticism*.

3. Anonymous reviewer for *Times Literary Supplement*, in *The New English Bible Reviewed*, ed. Nineham, 74.

4. Raymond C. Van Leeuwen, "We Really Do Need Another Translation," *Christianity Today*, October 22, 2001, 30.

5. Anonymous, in *The New English Bible Reviewed*, ed. Nineham, 75.

6. Martin Jarrett-Kerr, "Old Wine: New Bottles," in *The New English Bible Reviewed*, ed. Nineham, 125.

7. F. L. Lucas, review of NEB, in *Literary Style of the Old Bible and the New*, ed. D. G. Kehl (Indianapolis: Bobbs-Merrill, 1970), 50.

8. T. S. Eliot, review of NEB in the *Sunday Telegraph*, in *Literary Style of the Old Bible and the New*, ed. Kehl, 54.

9. Lucas, in *Literary Style,* ed. Kehl, 52.

10. Eliot, in *Literary Style*, ed. Kehl, 56.

11. Jarrett-Kerr, in *The New English Bible Reviewed*, ed. Nineham, 122.

12. Dwight Macdonald, "The Bible in Modern Undress," in *Literary Style*, ed. Kehl, 38.

13. Dorothy Thompson, "The Old Bible and the New," in *Literary Style*, ed. Kehl, 45.

14. Eliot, in *Literary Style*, ed. Kehl, 56.

15. C. L. Wrenn, review of NEB in *Studia Evangelica*, in *The New English Bible Reviewed*, ed. Nineham, 136.

16. V. S. Pritchett, "The Finalised Version," in *Literary Style*, ed. Kehl, 62.

17. Macdonald, in *Literary Style*, ed. Kehl, 38.

18. Henry Gifford, in *The New English Bible Reviewed*, ed. Nineham, 110.

19. Jarrett-Kerr, in *The New English Bible Reviewed*, ed. Nineham, 123.

20. Gifford, in *The New English Bible Reviewed*, ed. Nineham, 110.

21. Jarrett-Kerr, in *The New English Bible Reviewed*, ed. Nineham, 126.

22. Pritchett, in *Literary Style*, ed. Kehl, 62.

23. Jarrett-Kerr, in *The New English Bible Reviewed*, ed. Nineham, 126.

24. Macdonald, in *Literary Style*, ed. Kehl, 38.

25. Stanley Edgar Hyman, " 'Understanded of the People,' " in *Literary Style*, ed. Kehl, 58.

26. John Livingston Lowes, "The Noblest Monument of English Prose," in *Essays in Appreciation* (Boston: Houghton Mifflin, 1936), 24–25.

27. Gifford, in *The New English Bible Reviewed*, ed. Nineham, 108.

28. Jarrett-Kerr, in *The New English Bible Reviewed*, ed. Nineham, 124.

29. Henry Seidel Canby, "A Sermon on Style," in *Literary Style*, ed. Kehl, 26.

30. Wrenn, in *The New English Bible Reviewed*, ed. Nineham, 138.

31. Ibid., 136.

32. Macdonald, in *Literary Style*, ed. Kehl, 40.

33. Hyman, in *Literary Style*, ed. Kehl, 58–59.

Chapter Eleven: The Content of the English Standard Version

1. J. I. Packer, "The Adequacy of Human Language," in *Inerrancy*, ed. Norman L. Geisler (Grand Rapids, MI: Zondervan, 1979), 211.

2. Gerald Hammond, *The Making of the English Bible* (New York: Philosophical Library, 1982), 2.

3. Ibid., 2.

4. Ibid., 12.

5. Raymond C. Van Leeuwen, "We Really Do Need Another Bible Translation," *Christianity Today*, October 22, 2001, 31.

Chapter Twelve: The Language and Style of the English Standard Version

1. Alister McGrath, *In the Beginning: The Story of the King James Bible and How It Changed a Nation, a Language, and a Culture* (New York: Anchor Books, 2001), 308–10.

2. David Curzon, *The Gospels in Our Image: An Anthology of Twentieth-Century Poetry Based on Biblical Texts* (New York: Harcourt Brace, 1995), xxxi.

3. Gordon D. Fee and Mark L. Strauss, *How to Choose a Translation for All Its* [sic] *Worth* (Grand Rapids, MI: Zondervan, 2007), 27.

4. John Bartlett, ed., *Bartlett's Bible Quotations* (New York: Little, Brown, 2005).

5. Leland Ryken, *Understanding English Bible Translation* (Wheaton, IL: Crossway, 2009), 122–25.

Chapter Thirteen: Rhythm and Fluency in the English Standard Version

1. F. L. Lucas, "The Greek 'Word' Was Different," in *Literary Style of the Old Bible and the New*, ed. D. G. Kehl (Indianapolis: Bobbs-Merrill, 1970), 51.

2. Dorothy Thompson, "The Old Bible and the New," in *Literary Style,* ed. Kehl, 46.

Chapter Fourteen: The English Standard Version as a Literary Bible

1. John Livingston Lowes, "The Noblest Monument of English Prose," in *Essays in Appreciation* (Boston: Houghton Mifflin, 1936), 7.

2. Eugene A. Nida, *Good News for Everyone* (Waco, TX: Word, 1977), 9–10.

3. Francis A. Schaeffer, *Art and the Bible* (Downers Grove, IL: InterVarsity, 1973), 38, 41.

GENERAL INDEX

SCRIPTURE INDEX

With so many Bible translations available, how do you make a choice between them?

As an expert in English literature and literary theory, Leland Ryken establishes the context for understanding contemporary English Bible translation theory and practice, and the effects upon our interpretation of God's Word.

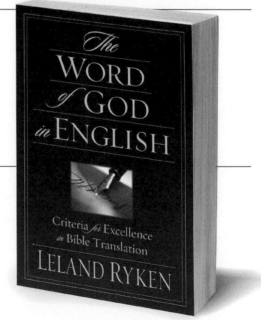

AN EXPERT, UP-TO-DATE CLARIFICATION OF THE ISSUES UNDERLYING
MODERN BIBLE TRANSLATION

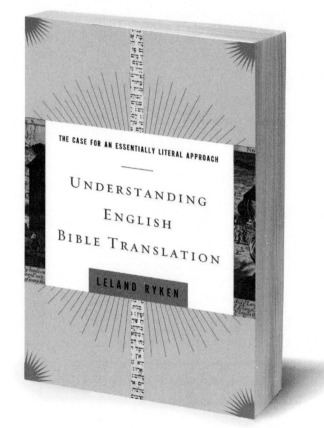

THE CASE FOR AN ESSENTIALLY LITERAL APPROACH

UNDERSTANDING

ENGLISH

BIBLE TRANSLATION

LELAND RYKEN

Provides a clear path through the maze of English Bible translations, defining the issues, contrasting the main traditions of modern Bible translation, and making a strong case for an essentially literal translation philosophy.

Modern Bible translations are at a crossroads. Multiple translation philosophies argue that there is a right way and a wrong way to translate the Bible. But who is right? And what has been the historic view of English Bible translators?

Leland Ryken, an expert on the literature of the Bible, brings clarity to these questions as he traces the history of English Bible translation from William Tyndale to the King James Bible and argues that the English Standard Version is the true heir of this classical stream.

Here is a great resource for Christians who have questions about why we have different Bible translations and how to choose between them.

"Leland Ryken brilliantly demonstrates historically and linguistically that Bible translation philosophy is a life and death matter. Unflinching. Powerful. Convincing."

R. KENT HUGHES, *Senior Pastor Emeritus, College Church, Wheaton, Illinois*

"An excellent book for understanding why translations differ and why it is important."

WAYNE GRUDEM, *Research Professor of Theology and Biblical Studies, Phoenix Seminary*

"In the current climate of pop Bible translations, it is critical to have a translation like the ESV, which is faithful to the original text, honors the traditional treasures of literary style and readability, and is widely accessible."

JON MCNEFF, *Senior Pastor, NorthCreek Church, Walnut Creek, California*

LELAND RYKEN is professor of English at Wheaton College and has written or edited numerous books, including *Understanding English Bible Translation, The Dictionary of Biblical Imagery,* and *The Legacy of the King James Bible.* Ryken served as literary stylist for *The Holy Bible, English Standard Version*®.

BIBLE REFERENCE

www.crossway.org

ISBN-13: 978-1-4335-3066-1
ISBN-10: 1-4335-3066-X

5 1 4 9 9

U.S. $14.99